Authentic Marketing

Authentic Marketing

How to Capture Hearts and Minds
Through the Power of Purpose

Larry Weber

WILEY

Cover image: © Max Krasnow/Shutterstock
Cover design: Wiley

Published by John Wiley & Sons, Inc., Hoboken, New Jersey.
Published simultaneously in Canada.

For general information on our other products and services or for technical support, please contact
our Customer Care Department within the United States at (800) 762–2974, outside the United
States at (317) 572–3993 or fax (317) 572–4002.

Wiley publishes in a variety of print and electronic formats and by print-on-demand. Some material
included with standard print versions of this book may not be included in e-books or in print-on-
demand. If this book refers to media such as a CD or DVD that is not included in the version you
purchased, you may download this material at http://booksupport.wiley.com. For more information
about Wiley products, visit www.wiley.com.

*Library of Congress Cataloging-in-Publication Data has been applied for and is on
file with the Library of Congress.*

ISBN 9781119513759 (Hardcover)
ISBN 9781119513735 (ePDF)
ISBN 9781119513773 (ePub)

Printed in the United States of America
V10006303_112118

To my family,
Your love and support I carry with
me every day. Thank you.

—LW

Contents

Foreword

For the past 15 years, I have had the pleasure of running companies that specialize in leadership networks and professional networking, giving me the unique opportunity to meet literally hundreds of Fortune 500 executives. I've had the privilege to hear first-hand their aspirations, fears, leadership philosophies, and challenges in an era that is unprecedented in its speed and scale—where technology has upended the way we interact, buy, operate, and sell.

Through this experience, it has become clear that companies and leaders are in a furious race to stay relevant, and it is no longer good enough to just make money. Operating with ethics, making judgment calls with a social conscience, and staying authentically relevant are critical for survival in business today. Yielding more than increased sales and shareholder wealth is now a key element of that imperative.

Fast forward to the present, where I am now in the thriving hub of Cambridge, Massachusetts, with the amazing opportunity of serving as CEO of Reputation Institute, the data-driven reputation advisory firm. In this new role, I was invited to chat with one of the legends in the universe of PR and brand management—Larry Weber—to exchange ideas on the need for companies to "infuse a sense of purpose into the soul of their organization." It was a very intriguing and timely discussion, given that we are embarking into an era of corporate mistrust where consumers are crying out for companies to take the lead in doing good for the world—while also delivering on their goods and services. As the leading company in the domain of mining, measuring, and managing reputation, and as a purveyor of reputation intelligence, Reputation Institute has a deep understanding and expertise in this realm.

As we were having our exploratory conversations, Larry was deep into the throes of writing *Authentic Marketing: How to Capture Hearts and Minds Through the Power of Purpose*. This is his sixth book, and it offers readers the opportunity to discover the critical role of moral purpose for companies and to better understand the need to integrate core competencies, business operations, technology, and engagement strategies around that purpose. What struck me in our discussions about the book—and the topic of using purpose as a central guiding principle for companies—was the inspiring and fluid way in which Larry engages with concepts of ethics, morality, integrity, and purpose. He feels it, knows it, and sees the gaps that marketers, brand owners, and C-suite executives need to fill to embrace it. It is no longer a world where the purpose of a company is merely rhetoric or represented by a poster of platitudes with no sense of direction, alignment, or commitment to deliver on it.

Larry has seen with clarity the inspiring movie in 3D vision where companies use purpose effectively to elevate their brands, stakeholder engagement, and long-term value to new levels … but he has also witnessed the flip side of when companies don't. His book encapsulates these experience-driven insights that help organizations discover the intersection of profit and purpose.

The subject of using purpose to drive decision making is key to companies and their leadership teams—and has become a strategic imperative in *remaining relevant* for future employees, customers, investors, and influencers. Staying relevant means keeping up with trends, adapting to new environments, and constantly reinventing your business by taking mental shortcuts to act upon large amounts of information and embrace new ways of thinking. For leaders, marketing and brand professionals and their colleagues, infusing purpose into the soul of your business is an inspirational *raison d'être* that should guide decision making, drive actions, and motivate companies to rethink how they tell their stories, the channels through which they deliver them, and the way they use data and technology to do so. Larry guides the reader to think about the potential revenue impact of a successfully demonstrated commitment to purpose and highlights the importance of storytelling and visual expression that is relevant for the world we live in today.

Larry brings a wealth of knowledge, connections, and foresight to the topic of purpose. He has the trust of global clients who have shared their stories with him and the undisputed wisdom as someone who has been at the frontier of building brand and marketing ecosystems for years. As a leader, he has not only proven his own ability to help clients stay relevant with his firm's focus on technology, but also has a track record of predicting those trends that define the future.

Kylie Wright-Ford, CEO, Reputation Institute

Acknowledgments

Writing books evokes profound appreciation. I am grateful to the many who took the time to share their thoughts and experiences with me, further developing my initial observations into themes and, ultimately, chapters. First and foremost I would like to thank Laura Feng, a writing partner extraordinaire! Thank you with all of my heart.

I would also like to thank all those who gave their generous time and insights: Andrea Wood (Best Buy), Matt Furman (Best Buy), Diana O'Brien (Deloitte), Andy Frawley (V12 Data), Mark Fuller (Rosc Global), Tony Cervone (General Motors), Dianne Ledingham (Bain & Company), Wendy Miller (Bain & Company), Jon Iwata (IBM), Alex Jutkowitz (Hill + Knowlton), Jeff Bradach (Bridgespan), Stephen Hahn-Griffiths (Reputation Institute), Kylie Wright-Ford (Reputation Institute), Jay Manson (Reputation Institute), Vicki Adang (John Wiley & Sons), Richard Narramore (John Wiley & Sons), Jeff Grogan (Racepoint Global), Brenda Littlefield (Racepoint Global), and Seth Hatfield (Racepoint Global).

Finally, a standing ovation to all the clients and colleagues I have worked with over the years who have helped build a narrative that is only getting richer because of you.

Larry

Introduction

Almost 40 years ago, I began a career in marketing, not knowing where it would take me. Today, the answer is clear. *Authentic Marketing* is the result of a series of evolutionary changes brought about by digital communications, social media, and the Internet, along with a generational mandate that companies operate with strong values, more humanity, and a moral purpose to do good for the world.

Companies today have an unprecedented opportunity to transform their businesses around a purpose that is a true extension of their DNA. It's the intersection of where profit meets purpose and the essence of doing well by doing good. As they discover a new foundation in moral purpose, their stories will be told and shared in a powerful light with transparency and impact, which is the heart of authentic marketing. Through this, they'll experience deeper and more meaningful engagement with customers, as well as attract a workforce motivated by purpose. Most importantly, they'll find these efforts will not only enhance their long-term value, but also make a difference in the world, which is the answer to society's ask.

I sincerely hope companies everywhere will embrace this change and we collectively can reinvent good around the world.

Larry Weber
Boston, Massachusetts

Authentic Marketing and the Power of Purpose

CHAPTER

1

Profit Meets Purpose

Find Your Company's Soul

E very so often the business world awakens to a new reality. We're in the midst of one today that directly addresses a question keeping most CEOs up at night: How do I deliver long-term, sustainable value that motivates employees, engages customers, strengthens my brand, and delivers the profitability my stakeholders demand? The answer is simple, yet transformative. As we move through the 21st Century, companies need to find their moral purpose—something that lives within the soul of their business, which can translate into a form of good that is beneficial to both their bottom line and to mankind. Profit meets purpose . . . the clarion call of today.

Companies rising to answer this call are well positioned to become the iconic brands that define this era, which has moved beyond digital to one of social consciousness. Proof of this profound shift came from a surprising call to action from BlackRock CEO Laurence Fink in his 2018 annual letter to CEOs, which sent shock waves through the financial community:

> Society is demanding that companies, both public and private, serve a social purpose. To prosper over time, every company must not only deliver financial performance, but also show how it makes a positive contribution to society. . . . Without a sense of purpose, no company, either public or private, can achieve its full potential. It will ultimately lose the license to operate from stakeholders.[1]
>
> *Laurence Fink, BlackRock CEO*

As the head of a firm that manages more than $6 trillion in investments, this influential investor is completely changing the dialogue and, in the process, sounding the alarm to the C-suite. "It may be a watershed moment on Wall Street, one that raises all sorts of questions about the very nature of capitalism. . . . But for the world's largest investor to say it aloud—and declare that he plans to hold companies accountable—is a bracing example of the evolution of corporate America," said *New York Times* columnist Andrew Ross Sorkin.[2] He added that Fink's argument in part rests on the changing mood of the country regarding social responsibility.

Proving that point are findings from an April 5, 2018, Covestro survey of U.S. Fortune 1000 CEOs on business and purpose.[3] The survey found that a full 69% of senior executives say the act of balancing profit and purpose is having a positive, transformational impact on business, with half or more reporting such impacts as they integrate a purpose-driven approach into various functions. Four out of five (80%) agree that a company's future growth and success will hinge on a values-driven mission that balances profit and purpose, and 75% believe these types of companies will have a competitive advantage over those that do not.

Beyond CSR

What we're talking about here is a reinvented good, which is markedly different from simply implementing a traditional CSR effort—typically a siloed initiative that is completely separate from a company's business focus, product development, marketing, etc. By contrast, this "better good" is central to the organization's core mission. It is a fundamental value that is infused into the company's bloodstream so that it runs horizontally through every facet of the business—from R&D and marketing to finance and HR.

Discovering a moral mission requires a little soul searching. Typically, it involves an exercise that serves to identify an intrinsic value embedded in a company's DNA, which is a logical extension of the business that can do good for the world. The end of this chapter provides an exercise on this process, but I'll offer the example below to help bring it to life.

A few years back, I asked Sam Allen, chairman and CEO, Deere & Company, what he wanted his legacy to be at this venerable company, which has been in operation since 1837. His answer was not to simply sell more green tractors than the previous CEO. His vision was to, yes, continue to have Deere deliver profitability to stakeholders by selling plenty of those machines, but moreover to elevate the brand by delivering a higher value to its customers and the world. The strategy, which moved Deere into an entirely different category than its competitors, was to use software to enable farmers to maximize their yield, ultimately helping them feed an ever-growing planet. With the population expected to grow by two billion, this enabled Deere to address a major world issue. This was Deere's moral purpose.

This purposeful moral path is analogous to Aristotle's eudaimonia, a Greek word that often is translated to mean the state of having a good in-dwelling spirit. Aristotle's concept was that a man who possesses excellence or virtue in character does the right thing at the right time and in the right way. Similarly, companies that follow this path of "right" will prosper on multiple levels, as it will fuel business prosperity and deliver an entirely new level of engagement with stakeholders.

Deloitte sets an excellent example of a large, global network that is embracing this new form of good. I spoke with Diana O'Brien, Deloitte global chief marketing officer, about the company's robust WorldClass, 50 million futures initiative, which is focused on empowering millions who have been left behind to succeed through education and training.

What makes Deloitte unique is the belief that we're really only as good as the good we do. We empower our more than 260,000 people around the network to go out and make an impact that matters for clients, people, and communities. Professionals are asked to share their core skills and experiences to reach the goal of preparing 50 million futures for a world of opportunity. That's the rallying cry. It's accessible, available to everyone, and understood around the globe.

Authentic Marketing: The Driver of True Engagement

What excites me most about this infusion of good into business strategy is that it creates a natural by-product of authentic marketing—the most powerful form of marketing I have witnessed in my entire career. Digital media and the Internet put us on this journey toward a more genuine form of marketing. These disruptive forces indelibly changed marketing from a one-way, shout-it-to-the-masses, no-listening environment, to a dialogue-driven, engagement-centric approach that put the power in the hands of consumers—where it belongs. The addition of moral purpose is the essential missing piece in this equation—the tipping point, if you will, that forges entirely new levels of engagement between companies and constituents.

Companies doing this new, deeper good will experience marketing that is far more transparent and organic, as it will be largely done at the hands of constituents who are eager to share positive stories across social channels. In this sense, they will serve to co-create companies' brands. It unleashes the true power of earned (social and traditional) media—the most important media, in my opinion, and also serves up powerful narratives for owned and paid media. Most importantly, it helps companies establish trust with constituents—the fundamental component of engagement and brand loyalty. Chapter 4 provides the essential skills of an authentic marketing program.

Good Momentum

Look around and you'll see this form of good is starting to take hold across all industries—from agriculture to automotive—and all around the world—from Beijing to Bangladesh.

Fortune, for example, has been covering this business phenomenon for the past three years in its Change the World list (with help from its partners at Shared Value Initiative) profiling more than 50 companies around the globe that are "doing well by doing good." These organizations use a profit model to solve a host of global problems, from climate change to world hunger. Companies are chosen based on three criteria: (1) measurable social impact on special societal problems, (2) business results of profitability and contribution to shareholder value, and (3) degree of innovation in its efforts and whether others are following the lead.

Among the companies in *Fortune's* September 2017 list is Unilever, the $30 billion Anglo-Dutch consumer products giant. The article highlights that what CEO Paul Polman is most excited about is the 1.8 million people who apply for a job there each year, many of whom are millennials. What's the appeal? You guessed it. Unilever's Sustainable Living Plan and its "bigger purpose" as a business are the primary draws among roughly 60% of applicants, who feel it gives them an opportunity to make a bigger difference in the world than they could do on their own.[4]

This example highlights another critical outcome of having a social purpose. It has strong appeal to not only the population in general, but millennials in particular—an audience more than 80 million strong that accounts for an estimated $1 trillion of current U.S. consumer spending, according to an article in the *HuffingtonPost*.[5] The article also notes that 73% of this generation is willing to pay extra for sustainable offerings. Moreover, a full 81% expect companies to make public declarations of their corporate citizenship.[6]

Covestro's survey on business and purpose found that 77% of new hires and 76% of current employees are the primary drivers of demand for purpose-driven companies, followed by customers. A full 86% of CEOs/C-suite executives confirmed that today's top talent is more inclined to work for companies with a demonstrated commitment to social issues compared to ones that don't.[7] This underscores that doing good is no longer a nice "extra," but an essential action that is expected of every company in every industry—one of the new requirements to attract top talent.

Another standout name on *Fortune's* Change the World list is the nation's largest retailer, Walmart.[8] According to *Fortune*, the company is using its muscle to make its supply chain greener by pushing its "tens of thousands of suppliers to gradually get rid of controversial chemicals, like formaldehyde in wood resin-based products, in about 90,000 household items." This effort is an extension of the retailer's longer-term sustainability campaign. The company has "diverted 82% of materials that used to be considered waste away from landfills, compared with 64% just a few years ago."

IBM: Legacy Values Working for Good

Technology giant IBM was also spotlighted on *Fortune's* list for its stellar efforts to close the STEM skills gap in public schools, addressing the shortage of highly skilled employees in America.

Recently, I had a fascinating interview with Jon Iwata, IBM senior vice president and chief brand officer, who currently chairs the company's newly created Values and Policy Advisory Board, which recommends policies and principles for IBM. Iwata frames our conversation on IBM's societal purpose by going back to the very early days of the company, demonstrating its deep roots of following a strong value system:

> The company was founded on fundamental beliefs, which can be traced back to Thomas Watson, Sr., who became IBM's first CEO in 1914. Like Steve Jobs, Richard Branson, and Phil Knight of today, Watson had deep beliefs about IBM's purpose and what it should stand for. He institutionalized those as the company's Basic Beliefs. Although that phrase has since passed out of our vocabulary for various reasons, the idea remains that our company is set apart by what it believes and stands for.
>
> For example, IBM's longstanding commitment to what most recognize as "diversity and inclusion" today goes back to the company's belief in "respect for the individual." That has always meant that we see an individual not as a man or woman. We don't see an individual based on race, ethnicity, or disability. And, therefore, we demonstrate respect for each individual and work to help each person fulfill his/her potential in society and in IBM. We're proud that IBM was the first major company to hire a disabled employee and the first to promote a woman to vice president.
>
> The idea that new technology creates societal implications is not new. For example, technology will always have an impact on jobs. Some occupations go away— typing pools have gone away, as have human "computers." However, entirely new occupations and jobs get created. Fifty years ago, were there coders and software engineers,

cybersecurity analysts, even CIOs? IBM has felt a responsibility to not only create new technology, but to also ensure that the new technology is adopted and applied in ways that earn trust. Helping people develop new skills is part of that. Today, we're doing it again with AI—what we call "new collar jobs."

Our view is not to say, "Don't worry about the jobs that go away." It's to understand requirements of the new jobs—and the new requirements of existing jobs, which are often overlooked. Moreover, it's to take the additional step of creating curriculums, of engaging educational institutions, whether its MIT or a high school in New York City, to create the new curriculum and teach new skills so that workers—young future workers like kids or existing workers—can move to the new.

We don't have to do that. We choose to do that. Is it the right thing to do? It's the right thing to do for IBM because we've always felt we do not just stop by creating the new technology. We go the additional step of anticipating and then addressing it so that we can have a positive impact.

Patagonia: Pioneering Sustainability

The term sustainability is almost synonymous with Patagonia, a true pioneer with a fierce dedication for the past 40 years to lead the clothing industry in the adoption of sustainable processes. On the company's website, you'll see its moral purpose embedded throughout every aspect of its business and articulated loud and clear in its mission: *Build the best product, cause no unnecessary harm, use business to inspire and implement solutions to the environmental crisis.*[9] Its latest initiative, Patagonia Action Works, is an environmental activist effort to get supporters more involved in politics. As an outdoor gear retailer, Patagonia is an obvious fit for doing good for the world, but any brand in any industry can and should find its moral purpose.

Smaller companies are popping up all over that are launched with a moral mission. For example, on a recent trip to London, I walked into a store called Gandys. As soon as I entered, the sales person told me the story of the brand—a business created by two siblings who, while traveling the world with their parents, sadly lost them during the tsunami in Sri Lanka. These orphan siblings later formed Gandys in honor of their parents and to support their "Orphans for Orphans" foundation, which helps underprivileged children affected by the tsunami. The salesperson told this moving story before she mentioned the current sale or anything about the merchandise because it was—first and foremost—what the brand was all about. Guess how we reacted? We all wanted to buy a t-shirt, backpack, or sweater to support its mission.

The Call for Action-Driven Businesses

So why this and why now? It's simple. The world needs more good. People can no longer rely on government to solve some of the planet's thorniest problems, like world hunger, climate change, public health issues, and poverty . . . the list goes on. Yet, our planet has more complex problems than ever before. Because of that, people are looking to the private sector to step up, take action, and address issues that matter most to them. This is the thrust of Fink's message to CEOs.

Many companies are doing this, some in unexpected ways. One example that stunned the business community and struck a nerve in the health care arena was the January 30, 2018, announcement that Amazon, Berkshire Hathaway, and JPMorgan Chase & Co. are partnering to form an independent health care company for their U.S. employees.[10] This new organization is being formed to address a pressing issue in health care—helping people find "simplified, high quality and transparent health care at a reasonable cost," according to the press release. This unprecedented move illustrates how companies are moving into nontraditional territory, taking on bold new initiatives to address frustrating problems that are a top priority.

Another example is a company taking action following the devastating Parkland, Florida, shooting in February 2018. Dick's Sporting Goods was among several companies that took an anti-gun stance and changed its policies. The company announced it would stop selling assault-style rifles and high-capacity magazines and pushed for gun control measures in Congress. The stock market showed its approval with shares closing up.

A New Strategy Model for a New Era

For purpose to be a great transformer in any organization, it requires not just new thinking, but an entirely retooled business model involving a broader definition of strategy. Chapter 3 outlines the elements of this tightly integrated model. This model will disrupt the highly siloed approach, in which a company develops a business strategy first and then separate strategies for all other departments, an approach that has been in existence for decades. The new strategy fuses a tight integration across all of these critical pillars of business with purpose as the glue that binds them.

While the concept of purpose is in vogue right now, this is by no means a flash-in-the-pan trend. I believe this is a core strategic driver that will become a permanent element of business strategy. Simply put, it is now an ethical responsibility for companies to integrate good into their overall strategies.

Soul Searching: Exercise to Find Your Moral DNA

In my work to help companies identify their moral purpose, I've found that people have very different reactions. For some, an obvious answer will surface immediately. For others, the concept feels overwhelming. In both cases, the exercise outlined below will provide clarity. If you think you have a great idea, this process will serve as a reality check. If you aren't sure how to start, it will put you on the path of discovery.

Key to this process is remembering this: *the purpose you identify should be a natural and logical extension of your business—something embedded in the DNA of your organization.* I bring this up again because when this purpose is truly at the heart of your company and its values, something that's a natural fit, it will take hold, have staying power, and deliver as it should, impacting both the success of your business and of your mission to do good.

I'll give a few examples to provide context and ignite your thinking. A company that develops drones, for example, might find a way to put those mini aircrafts to work for disaster relief. A pharmaceutical company that develops drugs to help people with diabetes could fund research to help find a cure or shed light on new nutrition strategies. A business that develops steel might work to find a cleaner, more sustainable manufacturing process. I've yet to work with an organization that could not find a moral purpose that was a natural extension of its business. In most cases, it's an intuitive answer.

The process is actually quite straightforward and involves asking a series of questions around key topics: your company legacy and values, your audience, your offerings, and pressing issues associated with your business, products, or services. Your moral mission will be born out of integrating the answers.

Step One: Explore Values

Start by looking at your company's values. These could include a set of values developed recently to fit the times or legacy values the company was founded upon. Think about the IBM story. The company was founded with Basic Beliefs that included Respect for the Individual. That concept is a key driver of its efforts today, which earned IBM a prominent spot in *Fortune's* Change the World list. IBM took that core value and aligned it with initiatives that were a natural extension of its business. It worked to help create new curriculums and engage educational institutions so they could teach new skills, enabling workers to move into new jobs that technology had created. So, rather than technology replacing humans, this was an effort to help people keep pace with technology and prepare for new career opportunities offered by those innovations. Pursuing a moral purpose based on company values ensures the effort is anchored in something real and meaningful that is already woven into the fabric of the organization. This is the most critical element of the exercise.

Key Questions

- Does our company have a founding or current core value that is relevant to our audiences today?
- Can this core value become the driving force of an effort that is a natural extension of my business, which can have a positive impact on the world?

Step Two: Pay Products and Services Forward

Think about your core offerings. Perhaps there is a way to put your products or services to work for people in the world who need them most. For example, Microsoft is on a mission to "empower every person and every organization on the planet to achieve more," and is putting forth a variety of lobbying and partnering efforts to bring Internet access to the 24 million Americans who don't have it.[11] Called the Rural Airband Initiative, it will also bring software (such as Microsoft's own) to those who have no access. Other examples are TOMS' One for One® program in which the company donates a pair of shoes to children in need for every pair it sells. Warby Parker's Buy a Pair, Give a Pair, which involves giving a pair of glasses to people in need for every pair sold, is another great example. Finding creative ways to help mankind or the planet with your offerings is a powerful, natural extension of your business.

Key Questions

- Who in the world would most benefit if they had access to our product/service?
- How can we set up a program to provide access to our product/service to those people in need?

Step Three: Feed Your Audiences' Passions

If you are truly engaged and listening to your customers, you can easily identify what they care about most. I'm talking about concerns and/or passions they have about the world, whether it's climate change, family, education, nutrition, equality, or caring for those less fortunate. Your moral mission may involve putting your organization and its products/services to help in those plights.

Patagonia is a great example here. The company's customers are passionate about the outdoors and the environment, so creating sustainable materials that are good for the planet was an obvious and natural path. Another great example comes from Nestlé. The company has a robust nutrition effort in place with a goal of helping 50 million children lead healthier lives by 2030.[12] As part of this effort, the company conducted a ground-breaking study on the biology of growing children to understand who is at risk for certain diseases and how nutrition might help prevent the onset of those conditions. As part of this exercise, think about issues impacting your customers, and perhaps this can guide your moral compass.

Key Questions

- What do our customers care deeply about that is aligned with our business?
- How can we make a true difference in this area? What is needed most and how can we make an ongoing contribution?

Step Four: Take a Stand

Perhaps you develop a product or service offering (or are in some way associated with products or services) that has a potentially negative impact on society. These situations can present an opportunity to take a stand to ensure your products or services are used in a positive way rather than doing harm.

Today, companies can no longer be agnostic. They are expected to step up, take action, and address issues. For example, as I write this book, Facebook is at the center of a privacy scandal because it sold data from more than 50 million users to Cambridge Analytica. How the company handles this crisis will impact its brand and its business.

As an aside, I believe that with any innovation, new issues will arise that we have never dealt with before. The important thing is not *that* issues arise, but rather *how* those issues are handled. Companies need to be honest about what went wrong, take ownership when appropriate, and take action to help fix the problem. And they need to do all of this quickly. Silence lets others fill in the void and tell your story in their words, not yours.

Companies are stepping up in great numbers today to take a stand on high-profile issues. I mentioned Dick's Sporting Goods' gun control efforts following the Parkland, Florida, school shooting earlier, but the company was not alone. L.L.Bean halted sales of guns and ammunition to anyone under the age of 21; the grocery store Kroger stopped selling assault-style rifles; and REI stopped selling products from Vista Outdoor because it owns Savage Arms, a company that manufactures guns.[13]

While this exemplifies a one-off stance on a pressing moral issue, it highlights what the world expects from companies today. It also shows how companies are moving out of the neutral zone and becoming action-oriented to change the world for the better. In addition to doing the right thing in moments like these to support worthy causes, companies should also have a larger moral mission tied to their DNA, an ongoing effort that is a natural extension of the brand.

One important footnote on this: if you choose to support more controversial issues (like immigration and gun control, as examples) know that you will be applauded by some and alienated by others. As such, you need assess the risks you take, understand the potential upsides and downsides of your actions, and know how your most important stakeholders will react.

According to a *Harvard Business Review* article,[14] you should "gauge how the social purpose idea both generates business value and minimizes the company's exposure to risk. An effective social-purpose strategy creates value by strengthening a brand's key attributes or building new adjacencies. At the same time, it mitigates the risk of negative associations among consumers and threats to stakeholder acceptance."

Key Questions

- Does our product or service hold the potential to do harm in any way (think security issues, environmental issues, job loss issues, etc.)?
- If the answer is yes, what type of effort can we initiate to be vigilant and proactive to ensure more good than harm comes from our offerings? Can we take a leadership role in this effort?
- If it is a controversial subject, what risks do we need to assess and where do we need alignment?

Once you have answers to the above questions, review them to determine which moral mission best fits within your organization's DNA. Then assess each to identify which one would have the most positive impact on your stakeholders and the planet, while also delivering long-term value to your business.

One final note about traditional CSR efforts and their place in this new equation: If your company has been generously donating to worthy causes or funding important efforts, such as building a new hospital or putting a new park in your community, you do not have to put a halt to those worthy initiatives. The world needs those types of giving-back contributions as well. Moving forward, however, find ways to tie those types of giving-back initiatives into your larger moral mission so that it becomes an extension of it, making it stronger and more meaningful.

Notes

1. Larry Fink's Letter to CEOs, www.blackrock.com/corporate/investor -relations/larry-fink-ceo-letter
2. *New York Times*, "BlackRock's Message: Contribute to Society, or Risk Losing Our Support," January 15, 2018, www.nytimes.com/2018/01/15 /business/dealbook/blackrock-laurence-fink-letter.html
3. Covestro unveils new survey of U.S. Fortune 1000 CEOs on business and purpose, April 5, 2018.www.prnewswire.com/news-releases /covestro-unveils-new-survey-of-us-fortune-1000-ceos-on-business 1-and-purpose-300624494.html
4. *Fortune*, Change the World 2017, September 15, 2017, page 75, http:// fortune.com/2017/09/07/change-the-world-money/
5. *Huffington Post*,blog, "Corporate Social Responsibility Matters: Ignore Millennials at Your Peril," 2/5/16, www.huffingtonpost.com/ryan -rudominer/corporate-social-responsi_9_b_9155670.html
6. *Forbes*, "Millennials Driving Brands to Practice Socially Responsible Marketing," 3/17/17, www.forbes.com/sites/sarahlandrum/2017/03/17 /millennials-driving-brands-to-practice-socially-responsible-marketing /#742905694990
7. Covestro unveils new survey of U.S. Fortune 1000 CEOs on business and purpose, April 5, 2018.www.prnewswire.com/news-releases /covestro-unveils-new-survey-of-us-fortune-1000-ceos-on-business -and-purpose-300624494.html
8. *Fortune*, Change the World 2017, September 15, 2017, page 79
9. Patagonia, www.patagonia.com/company-info.html
10. Amazon, Berkshire Hathaway, and JPMorgan Chase & Co. to partner on U.S. employee healthcare, Press Release, January 30, 2018, www .businesswire.com/news/home/20180130005676/en/Amazon-Berkshire -Hathaway-JPMorgan-Chase-partner-U.S.

11. *Fortune*, Change the World 2017, September 15, 2017, page 83

12. Nestlé,www.nestle.com/stories/helping-kids-lead-healthier-lives

13. *Business Insider*, LL Bean, REI and Dick's Update Gun Control Policies, March 2, 2018, www.businessinsider.com/ll-bean-rei-and-dicks-update -gun-control-policies-2018-3

14. *Harvard Business Review*, "Competing on Social Purpose," September– October 2017, https://hbr.org/2017/09/competing-on-social-purpose

CHAPTER

2

The Era of Social Consciousness

Where Technology Meets Humanity

The past few decades have been defined by a relentless stream of innovations in technology, many of which have blown in like a bomb cyclone, churning up industries and companies, creating new ones, and destroying others in the process. Never before in history has the cadence of change been so swift or dramatic.

In just a few short decades, technology has evolved from a back-end solution to a ubiquitous element that is as engrained in our lives as the air we breathe. Earlier waves (think mainframes, PCs, client/server computing, the Internet, among others) were primarily about enhancing business productivity and providing information at your fingertips. More recent innovations (social media, IoT, voice recognition, search technology, and the second coming of AI, as examples), however, brought about dramatic new dynamics in communications, connectedness, convenience, personalization, security, and automation. This wave of technology largely focused on individuals, with offerings that made life richer, easier, more convenient, and safer.

When you think about it, it's astonishing. It wasn't all that long ago that the idea of carrying a device in your pocket that would enable you to access every kind of information imaginable, take photos, quickly communicate in real time with people anywhere in the world, measure your heart health, and adjust the temperature in your home, would sound more like an episode from The Jetsons than a possible reality. But, on January 9, 2007, Steve Jobs launched the iPhone at Macworld, giving the world "a widescreen iPod with touch control, a revolutionary phone, and a breakthrough Internet communications device." "Are you getting it?" Jobs said on stage. "These are not three separate devices. This is one device."[1] That one device has changed the world. Since that day, Apple has sold more than one billion iPhones.[2] Incredible.

Amazon has become the standard by which we judge shopping experiences. By maximizing technologies such as AI/machine learning, image/voice recognition, and algorithms, the company serves up incredible convenience, personalized recommendations, chatbot-based customer service, fast search results, and excellent product recommendations.[3] Netflix has redefined how we are entertained in our homes, enabling us to binge watch programs without being interrupted by ads. And can you imagine life without Google? Think about how many times a day you use it to find an answer to a question—literally any question that's on your mind.

Wearable technologies now help us do everything from monitor our health to enhance our workouts. Today there are wristbands that monitor your heart rate and send real-time information to your doctor; smart shoes that feature a fitness tracker in the soles; smart watches that put smartphone capabilities on your wrist; and smart bike helmets with a collision detection feature that sends a message to a loved one if you are in an accident. Personal assistants like Google Home and Alexa do everything from making grocery lists to streaming music to reading the news and controlling things like lights and appliances in smart homes.

Social Media, Cultural Game Changer

Without a doubt, one of the biggest impacts on our culture has been social media, changing everything about how we communicate as a society, how companies engage with customers, and who is in the driver's seat. Although Facebook has certainly had to confront serious issues related to data privacy, no one can deny the universal connectivity this platform has brought to the more than two billion people around the world who use it.

Think back only to the late 1990s/early 2000s and the powerful role advertising played in companies' marketing communications strategies. It seems absolutely archaic now to think that organizations relied so heavily (and invested so much) in that one-way, megaphone form of communication that involved virtually no listening or conversations whatsoever.

Social media shifted the focus to dialogue and, along the way, has given consumers the loudest, most important voice in the mix, putting them squarely at the center of everything—where they should be. As social media shifted *the power* to the hands of consumers, their wants, needs, likes, dislikes, passions, opinions, and concerns about the world have taken center stage. Because of this, technology has helped set the scene for the era of social consciousness, which at its core is about *humanity*.

Let's take a closer look at some of the driving forces behind this.

The Call for Values

As the balance of power moved to customers, they are making it crystal clear what they expect from companies. Not only have they set a high bar for customer experience (CX), but they also have new mandates for company values and purpose . . . and they vote with their wallets. Their directive is for companies to become more genuine, more transparent, more likeable and operate every day with strong values—in a sense, to become more human *and* more humane. Companies that get it right will find their customers actually co-create their brands through their likes, shares, peer reviews, personal storytelling, etc.

Those that don't, however, will find that their bad behavior will be called out in a nanosecond, with reputations and stock values paying the price. We all remember United Airlines' misstep when it forcibly removed a passenger from his seat and dragged him down the aisle because he refused to give up his seat for an airline maintenance worker. Video footage spread like wildfire across the digital and broadcast landscapes, showcasing an ugly, inhumane side of the airline. As if that wasn't bad enough, the CEO then stepped in with a careless apology that did not in any way own up to the incident.

Guess what happened? United Airlines' stock took a nosedive, dropping initially by nearly 4% and knocking off close to $1 billion from the company's market value. Eventually, the CEO issued another, more appropriate apology and shares rebounded, but its market cap was still off by $250 million.[4] Ouch.

Starbucks had a negative video go viral involving the arrest of two black men who were waiting for a friend at one of its Philadelphia locations. The two men entered the coffee shop, asked to use the bathroom, were refused, and when they sat down without ordering anything, the manager called the police and had them arrested for trespassing. No charges were filed against the two men, but the court of public opinion found Starbucks guilty of racial bias. The company reacted promptly with a bold move of closing 8,000 stores for an afternoon in May 2018 to provide racial bias training to its employees.[5]

Another major misstep involves companies making false claims about their products. Crossing this line has cost businesses millions—in some cases billions—as well as their reputations. Volkswagen is a poster child of this form of bad behavior, with its false claims about its "clean diesel" vehicles. Dubbed "dieselgate," the company had rigged diesel vehicles to cheat emissions tests. Reports indicate the scandal has cost the company $30 billion in total.[6] Figure 2.1 illustrates Greenpeace activists protesting in front of the company's headquarters in Wolfsburg.[7] This photo, along with video footage, appeared in multiple

FIGURE 2.1   The public's strong reaction to "Dieselgate."
Source ET Auto, from the *Economic Times,* September 8, 2017

media outlets and was emblematic of the public's reaction to the scandal. It highlights the damage false claims can do a company's reputation, along with its finances.

That's just one example. Red Bull, Activia Yogurt, Airborne, Splenda, and countless others have the dubious distinction of having made false claims to customers. They all paid hefty price tags for these deceptive actions, with Red Bull paying out $13 million, including $10 to every U.S. consumer who bought the drink since 2002; Activia paid $45 million in a class-action lawsuit; Airborne paid $23.3 million in a class-action lawsuit and an additional $7 million settlement later; and Splenda's settlement amount is undisclosed.[8] On top of millions in lost revenues, misleading claims create broken trust with customers, who often move on to other brands.

The lesson in all of these examples is clear. Companies must follow their moral compass, treat people humanely and justly, and operate every day with honesty and integrity. This is what the world demands . . . and it is a fierce watchdog.

Higher Expectations of the Private Sector

As our government fails to step up to solve many of the world's complex problems, consumers also have made it clear they expect the private sector to not only operate with strong values, but to move out of being agnostic or neutral and take a stand to address world issues.

A 2017 study showed that 70% of Americans believe companies have an obligation to take action to improve issues that may not be relevant to their everyday business.[9]

Millennials, in particular, are more judgmental about the company they keep. This massive purpose-driven audience, one of the largest in history that is just reaching its prime spending years, is forcing organizations to take a hard look at their moral purpose to ensure they are making positive contributions to the world. Today, companies must not only create great products/ services, but also behave with greatness—with a generosity of giving back to mankind. I'll bring it back to Aristotle: they must act with eudaimonia in mind.

The demand for this comes not only from customers, but from employees as well. Today's top talent, especially millennials, seek to work for companies with a mission to do good for the world and to make a personal contribution to that effort. According to Covestro's survey on business and purpose, 68%

of Fortune 1000 CEOs say it is important for their companies to empower employees' sense of purpose. They predict that employee demand for purpose will increase over the next 10 years, primarily due to millennials and their mindset.[10]

Google is one example of a company that has moved forward with an initiative that gives Internet access to cities across Africa. CVS also made the bold move of taking cigarettes off of its shelves to help its customers quit smoking. It was a step that further established CVS as a wellness company. Larry J. Merlo, president and CEO of CVS Health, said, "Ending the sale of cigarettes and tobacco products at CVS/pharmacy is the right thing for us to do for our customers and our company to help people on their path to better health. Put simply, the sale of tobacco products is inconsistent with our purpose."[11]As you read on, you'll learn about scores of other companies that are embracing this new modus operandi.

Technology Innovations as a Force for Good

The plethora of technology available today holds so much potential to make our lives easier, more fulfilling, and more entertaining, to enhance our health and well-being, and to stay connected to new friends and old. Although there are also potential negatives with any technology, this underscores the importance of being vigilant to ensure it delivers more good than harm to the world. This is the intersection of technology and morality.

The "move fast and break things" mantra of Silicon Valley must adjust to find a balance between hyper-fast movement for the sake of breakthrough innovation and thoughtful consideration of any potential negative ramifications new technologies might have on society. This is particularly true as innovations come to market that can literally reshape our society and economy.

An article on MarketWatch summed up the critical questions technology companies must ask themselves today: "These challenges won't be strategic, financial, or technical, but instead will be more focused on philosophical, societal, and ethical questions. Questions like: What role does our technology play in society, and what responsibility do we, the creators of these innovations, have in shaping the societal and economic consequences that accompany them?"[12]

Companies are stepping up to address this higher purpose. For example, at the Viva Technology conference in Paris in May 2018, IBM CEO Ginni Rometty articulated her company's philosophy and principles around AI, which include "ensuring companies remember that data belongs to the person who created it, AI must be transparent and explainable, and it should be used to augment human intelligence, not replace it."[13]

The company also announced a "Call for Code" initiative, which is "the largest and most ambitious effort to bring startup, academic, and enterprise developers together to solve one of the most pressing societal issues of our time: preventing, responding to, and recovering from natural disasters." Its goal is to unite the world's developers and tap into data and AI, blockchain, cloud, and IoT technologies to address social challenges.[14]

This exemplifies how companies are working to not only ensure that technologies do no harm, but taking it further to determine how innovations can be used to help solve societal problems. Companies in every industry, not just technology, can and should use technology for social good. As we look at today's innovative technologies, so many of them have enormous potential in this realm.

I believe AI is one of most exciting and important technologies today as it enables game-changing happenings across many industries. AI is helping companies and products operate with more human-like smarts: recognizing faces; serving up suggestions when you shop; helping drivers to parallel park; putting paper towels on shopping lists; and even fueling smarter prosthetics. Increasing your security, creating better, more personalized experiences, and making life easier are some of the many benefits AI is delivering.

But AI also holds enormous potential to do good for the world. This technology can be used to improve everything from health care and environmental sustainability to protecting endangered wildlife, providing urban mobility and public welfare, and assisting in low resource communities.

According to an article in *Forbes*, AI combined with human ingenuity is helping us do good in new and better ways. Author Diane Melley of IBM states, "... I'm optimistic about bringing these new capabilities to bear against important problems like disease, natural disasters, aging populations, pollution and illiteracy. ... I can't help but think that AI, used wisely, might just be the social change catalyst of our lifetime."[15]

Many other technologies, such as mobile phone networks, the Internet, apps and software of all kinds, as well as data analytics, can and are being used to solve world problems. Here are a few quick examples:

- Johnson & Johnson launched a program in India that uses cell phone technology to send pregnant women and new moms voicemail messages on health-related topics and critical information about raising children.[16]
- Big data company SAS is leveraging data insight expertise to help crime fighters secure critical pieces of information.[17]

- Vodafone is extending e-commerce to African merchants by providing a payment system platform.[18]

Companies of all sizes across the globe are finding ways to leverage technology to power or amplify their moral missions. In this way, every company in every industry must embrace the mindset that they are indeed a technology company, applying the right innovations for not only their business strategies, but for their societal purpose as well.

All of these forces—consumers remaking corporate values, a generational mandate for helping the world, as well as technology innovations that can power good—define this purpose-driven landscape and, with it, the need for a new strategy model outlined in the next chapter.

Notes

1. *Time* magazine, Watch Steve Jobs Unveil the First iPhone 10 Years Ago Today, January 9, 2017, http://time.com/4628515/steve-jobs-iphone-launch-keynote-2007

2. *Forbes*, Apple Has Sold 1.2 billion iPhones Over the Past 10 Years, June 29, 2017, www.forbes.com/sites/niallmccarthy/2017/06/29/apple-has-sold-1-2-billion-iphones-over-the-past-10-years-infographic/#65a6fb7242f8

3. *Martech Today*, How E-commerce Giants Are Using AI and Marketing, November 22, 2017, https://martechtoday.com/ecommerce-giants-using-ai-marketing-part-1-207259

4. *CNN Money*, United Airlines Shares Drop After Man Dragged Off Flight, April 11, 2017, http://money.cnn.com/2017/04/11/investing/united-airlines-stock-passenger-flight-video/index.html

5. *Business Insider*, Starbucks' Baristas Respond to Plans for Racial-Bias Training, April 23, 2018, www.businessinsider.com/starbucks-racial-bias-training-what-baristas-think-2018-4

6. *CNN Money*, Volkswagen's Diesel Costs Hit $30 Billion, September 29, 2017, http://money.cnn.com/2017/09/29/investing/volkswagen-diesel-cost-30-billion/index.html

7. Gettyimages, www.gettyimages.co.uk/detail/news-photo/an-activist-holds-up-a-sign-reading-no-more-lies-during-a-news-photo/489941552#

/an-activist-holds-up-a-sign-reading-no-more-lies-during-a-protest-of
-picture-id489941552

8. *Business Insider*, 18 False Advertising Scandals, February 27, 2017, www.
businessinsider.com/false-advertising-scandals-2017–2#splenda-said-it
-was-made-from-sugar-15

9. 2017 Cone Communications CSR Study, https://static1.squarespace.
com/static/56b4a7472b8dde3df5b7013f/t/5947dbcf4f14bc4eadcd0
25d/1497881572759/CSRInfographic+FINAL2.jpg

10. Covestro unveils new survey of U.S. Fortune 1000 CEOs on business and purpose, April 5, 2018, www.prnewswire.com/news-releases
/covestro-unveils-new-survey-of-us-fortune-1000-ceos-on-business
-and-purpose-300624494.html

11. CVS Caremark to Stop Selling Tobacco at all CVS/Pharmacy Locations,
Feb. 5, 2014, www.prnewswire.com/news-releases/cvs-caremark-to-stop
-selling-tobacco-at-all-cvspharmacy-locations-243662651.html

12. MarketWatch, Facebook's Mark Zuckerberg Could Use a Chief Philosophy Officer, May 3, 2018, www.marketwatch.com/story/facebooks-mark
-zuckerberg-could-use-a-chief-philosophy-officer-2018–05–03

13. VentureBeat, IBM Ginni Rometty Calls on Developers to Embrace
Responsible AI Principles, May 24, 2018, https://venturebeat.com
/2018/05/24/ibm-ceo-ginni-rometty-calls-on-developers-to-embrace
-responsible-ai-principles

14. IBM News Room, IBM Leads "Call for Code" to Use Cloud, Data, AI,
Blockchain for Natural Disaster Relief, May 25, 2018, www-03.ibm.com
/press/in/en/pressrelease/54007.wss

15. *Forbes*, AI for Social Good: How Humans and Machines are Making a
Better World, April 11, 2107, www.forbes.com/sites/ibm/2017/04/11
/ai-for-social-good-how-humans-and-machines-are-making-a-better
-world/#4f7349e4370a

16. *Fortune*, Change the World 2017, September 15, 2017

17. *Fortune*, Change the World 2017, September 15, 2017

18. *Fortune*, Change the World 2017, September 15, 2017

A Better Strategy Model for a Better World

When BlackRock CEO Laurence Fink issued his clarion call, he elevated societal purpose from a topic that was bubbling under the surface to one that erupted onto everyone's radar and was pushed to the top of many company agendas. Many forces have converged to make this our new reality: a complex world with complex problems, a lack of faith in government to address those issues, and the loud voice of consumers, who increasingly call out for companies to demonstrate stronger values and contribute to society. Study after study prove that today's consumer—millennials in particular—prefer to buy products from and work for companies that are doing good for the world, underscoring that moral purpose drives long-term value. Without a doubt, this is the Zeitgeist of this era.

Organizations today will rise and fall based on their ability to deliver on these new demands. It's no longer enough to have a strong balance sheet and to create innovative products and services. Companies that succeed today will be those that find a path to become profitable through a purposeful mission. And while this concept has certainly started to take root, many are still holding tight to the old strategy model, which is in dire need of disruption.

"In an environment of constant change, rapid technological advances, social and demographic diversity, leaders can no longer rely on the toolbox of the past," said Nanette M. Blandin, a leadership scholar and president of the Nexus Institute, based in Washington, D.C.[1]

This landscape calls for a new strategic framework incorporating the new criteria necessary for success. The model proposed in this chapter is one where profit meets purpose, where technology fuels excellence, and where marketing becomes authentic—amplifying the good a company is doing and, along the way, creating deeper engagement with today's diverse constituencies, who can be bound together by purpose.

Shortcomings of the Current Model

Before we get into the new model, let's take a quick look at why the existing one is ripe for change. Historically, companies begin by developing an overarching business strategy. It is often a very linear, time-intensive process: research, develop plan, implement, measure, rinse, repeat. Once this plan is in place, companies then develop separate strategies for other key business functions like marketing, HR, manufacturing, etc. These efforts are often siloed without the benefit of integration. Even the physical space in offices often separate these functions, with HR in one hallway, marketing in another, and finance in yet another. In best-case scenarios, these siloed functions work to align with business strategies, so they share common goals. Software applications have forced horizontal integration across functions, but we must go further than that for true integration. In worst-case scenarios, they work as completely separate entities with little commonality and no integration. In all cases, it's a dated process ready for change.

I spoke with Mark Fuller, chairman of Rosc Global, co-founder of Monitor Group, now Deloitte Monitor, and former assistant professor at Harvard Business School. He shared his vast insights on the shortcomings of the current business strategy and how the new model delivers the type of framework necessary in today's business climate:

> I'm going to make two primary points about where today's approach to strategy falls short. The first is there's a non-trivial sin of omission with the concept of moral purpose.

The collective service industry is very active in three of the four pillars of your strategy (business, technology, and marketing), but doesn't deal with moral purpose, so it's defective in that realm. There has long been this issue between the client and the consultant not talking about moral issues because they are somehow not businesslike. They're embarrassing. And there are all kinds of reasons why. Numbers are okay to discuss because they're businesslike. So it's easy to show the client how much more revenue they're going to get, how much they'll save, their projected growth rates, predictions on the future size of their market. But there's been a resistance about discussing those embarrassing issues where you might have to use words like love or change the world or giving deep meaningfulness to what you do. It's not businesslike. So it's an easy sin to commit, but they're both doing the emperor's clothing routine.

Fuller continued, addressing the second major shortcoming:

Much of the service sector is also defective in that it delivers specialist content in various areas, but often leaves integration up to the clients who are left with all of these stovepipe specialist reports. They may be technically good, but the clients are sitting there with these piles of paper and saying, "How do I pull all of this together into an integrated whole for my company?" Since the number one thing that can provide coherence is the moral purpose piece and none of them are really doing that, they're not helping the client with the integrative balancing.

New thinking and the new requirements for success are starting to emerge in pockets throughout the business community. For example, the 2018 Deloitte Global Human Capital Trends Report emphasizes: "A profound shift is facing business leaders worldwide: The rapid rise of the social enterprise, reflecting the growing importance of social capital in shaping an organization's purpose, guiding its relationships with stakeholders, and influencing its ultimate success or failure."[2]

That same report also highlights the need for businesses to move toward integration: "The message is clear: Senior leaders must get out of their silos and work with each other more. To navigate today's constantly changing business environment and address cross-disciplinary challenges, a company's top leaders must act as one."[3]

Four Driving Principles of a New, Integrated Strategy Model

The new model eliminates the inefficient linear and siloed processes of the past. It fuses a tight integration of business, technology innovation, and engagement (marketing) strategies, all of which are bound together by a company's moral purpose (see Figure 3.1).

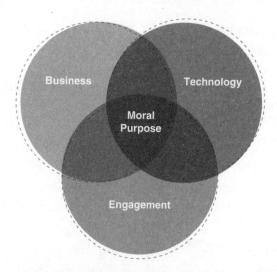

FIGURE 3.1 Moral purpose brings together a company's business, technology innovation, and engagement strategies. *Source* Racepoint Global

With "good" at the very center, it operates as the soul of the company, uniting and anchoring all strategies around a very real and powerful purpose. These strategies are all developed in unison so they are tightly aligned right from the start.

1. Business Strategy

The business strategy process is similar to traditional efforts. It could take an entire book to go through every detail of this process, but to top line it, the purpose is to determine why a company exists (business mission), what it strives to become in the world (business objectives), and how it's going to get there (strategies, tactics, and resources). This process involves a number of analyses (SWOT, competitive analysis, customer segments, market dynamics, and more), as well as developing a plan for profitability and differentiation.

Here are a few key elements that should be front and center when working through this process:

Use Customers to Drive Business Direction Put customers at the center of everything. A deep knowledge of your customers and human behavior in general will deliver key insights that can ignite new ideas, provide clarity around important decisions, and drive strategic directions. This speaks to the importance of listening closely to customers, getting their input and feedback to evolve products, expand into entirely new realms and change direction when necessary.

I think the greatest strength of Apple lies in its innate ability and fierce drive to create technology that is elegant, intuitive, useful, and fun. With a staggering 1.3 billion collective Apple devices (from iPhones to Macs to Apple TVs) in use today, it's safe to say that Apple has the finger on the pulse of its customers.[4] One of the critical moments underscoring this took place following the launch of the Apple II, which was widely successful but limited by its command line interface to run programs. Steve Jobs knew there was something better and went in search of it. While there are a few versions of this story, legend has it that Jobs found what he was looking for at Palo Alto Research Center (PARC), where the first mouse-driven graphical user interface (GUI) was being developed. This breakthrough GUI—with its ability to have people simply point and click on icons with a mouse—was the start of making computers nearly intuitive.[5] While Apple's initial attempts at using this technology were underwhelming (Lisa was underpowered and too expensive, and the Macintosh floundered at first), this ultimately put the company on the trajectory of developing intuitive and engaging technology that anyone could use. And virtually everyone did. Fast forward, and that elegant, friendly user interface marches all the way to today's iPhone, which is currently in use by more than 700 million people . . . and counting.[6]

Evolutionize Your Industry   I am a big proponent of evolutionary versus revolutionary offerings because I believe the majority of successful innovations typically evolve what's already out there to deliver a better next-generation solution. Truly revolutionary offerings—from the light bulb to the phonograph to the Internet to wireless broadcast—do happen, but those are few and far between. Companies that are successful at evolving their market segments have keen insights into market needs, take the best of what's already out there, and apply the best of what's new to push their industry to its next phase.

Even Henry Ford, who is widely mistaken to have invented the car, actually took existing inventions (the car and the assembly line) and perfected them to develop a vehicle affordable enough for the masses. He was one of the great evolutionaries.

I will build a motor car for the great multitude. It will
be large enough for the family, but small enough for the
individual to run and care for. It will be constructed of
the best materials, by the best men to be hired, after the
simplest designs that modern engineering can devise. But
it will be so low in price that no man making a good salary
will be unable to own one—and enjoy with his family the
blessing of hours of pleasure in God's great open spaces.[7]

Other examples of highly successful companies that leveraged
and evolved what's out there to dominate their markets are Google
(by some reports the twentieth search engine), which perfected
fast quality searches through its use of web crawlers, indexes, and
search algorithms, literally turning its name into a verb; Airbnb,
not the first, but the name synonymous with rental properties,
which leveraged the shared value model to connect people looking to rent their homes with those looking for accommodations;
and GE, which has a long history of innovation and successful
reinvention since its founding in 1892. By identifying new market
opportunities, the company has evolved from creating light bulbs
and supplying energy to building locomotives to creating x-ray
machines to building jet engines to offering digital industrial software solutions. Now that's a long history of evolution.

All Eyes on Evolution   Our world seems to be moving at the
speed of sound these days, with new technologies emerging continually and market dynamics changing constantly. Staying on
top of this is essential to avoid disruption. It's far too easy to miss
the boat on important trends. Even a big company like Microsoft
can have this type of blind spot, as it did when it missed centering
its offerings around the Internet. IBM also missed an important
dynamic when it initially ignored cloud computing. And remember

that story I told you about Apple finding the GUI at PARC? Well, it was actually owned by Xerox, which moved too slowly to capitalize on its creation. Eventually, it launched a product (Xerox Star), but it was "too little, too late."[8]

The lesson? While no one has a crystal ball, companies must have expert resources focused on the evolution of absolutely everything that could impact their business. They should be continually asking questions about the evolutions happening around them to ensure important trends are factored in to company strategies. Working with external industry analysts and business consultants can be helpful in this process, as a key part of their job is to help companies recognize the impact of these changes, find the holes in their strategies, and identify new opportunities.

2. Moral Purpose: Find Your Raison D'être

Although the process described above is familiar, here's where it takes a turn to infuse moral purpose. Once a company decides what it wants to be from a business perspective—whether it's a startup ready to evolve its marketplace or create a new market category, or an existing company redefining its market—the next critical step is to identify a moral purpose. This should come from the very core of an organization—something in its DNA that is a natural and logical extension of the business. When this purpose is truly within the soul of a company, it will gain traction, have staying power, and deliver impact, both to the world and to the well-being of your business. This is the essence of doing well by doing good.

I'll borrow the words of Mahatma Gandhi here: "You must be the change you want to see in the world." Companies must determine what change their business would be best equipped to impact and wrap that into the fabric of their organizations.

That change can be an electrifying catalyst for attracting and retaining talent, as well as motivating them every day. A full 76% of millennials consider a company's social and environmental commitments when deciding where to work and 64% won't take a job if a potential employer doesn't have strong corporate social responsibility (CSR) practices.[9]

"You have to motivate your employees to join, to stay, to learn, to do their work, to take risks and not just play electronic games while at their desks," said Fuller. "If you want high-end talent, they are going to apply a moral lens to your company and join those they think are at a minimum morally acceptable, but preferably moral champions.

"So many times when a company is faltering, management blames it on the execution. They say they have a strategy, they just don't execute on it. I prefer the term *action* over execution and I think it all comes down to that. You need to get people to *act* on your strategy in their daily jobs. I believe the linkage between an organization's moral purpose and the actions of its employees is a very direct one. If you can get people morally committed to your larger cause, they will go and do things they would never do if you just offered them a bit more money. So if your problem is execution, Mr. CEO, you've got to pay more attention to the moral thing and not the 2000 step action plan that no one can remember anyway because it's too complicated."

Moral Purpose in Action   A conversation I had with Robert Sundy, head of brands and marketing services at Whirlpool, illustrates this. When Whirlpool discovered that every day thousands of kids miss school because they don't have clean clothes to wear, it inspired the company to develop its Care Counts™ program. By installing washers and dryers in schools, the pilot program has already helped improve school attendance for more than 90% of tracked participants, 95% had more motivation in class, plus 89% of students got good grades.[10] This is just one effort Whirlpool has underway to help people and the planet through its offerings. The organization also donates appliances to Habit for Humanity, for example.

Tony Cervone, General Motors' senior vice president of global communications, explained how his company found its moral mission. It's a great story that shows how this effort should be tightly woven into a company's core competency:

> A small group of us were actively exploring this subject with our CEO, Mary Barra. We thought about the fact that while our vehicles provide the benefits of getting people from point A to point B and enabling them to live outside of the cities and establish communities in suburban or rural areas, there were also some unintended negative consequences. I'm talking about things like collisions, emissions, and congestion. Although these consequences were completely unintended, we felt a responsibility to work toward solving those issues. So by honestly and authentically looking at those facts, we found GM's cause, its purpose. It led us to our mission of working toward zero crashes, zero emissions, and zero congestion. One piece of that solution involves our commitment to doing multiple battery electric vehicles and multiple fuel cell electric vehicles. We've committed to having 20 vehicles by 2023, and I expect that number is conservative.

Other examples include pharma giant GlaxoSmithKline releasing drugs from patents in the least developed countries to lower drug prices in those areas, making the drugs more accessible to people who need them. It also re-invests a percentage of its profits in those areas to train health workers and build medical infrastructure.[11] Through its Mastercard Aid Network, Mastercard is making it easier for charities to get help to people who need it during natural disasters or in war-torn countries. The company distributes a version of its cards loaded with points that can be redeemed at various merchants for necessities like groceries, medicine, shelter, building materials, or even business supplies.[12]

The soul-searching exercise outlined in Chapter 1 provides a process that guides companies through this effort. To provide a quick recap, the exercise involves exploring a series of questions around the following:

- *Company Core Values:* Is there a founding or current value relevant today that can be a driving force in our moral purpose?
- *Products and Services:* Who in the world would benefit most from our offerings, and how can we set up a program to deliver on that?
- *Audience's Passions:* What do our customers care deeply about that is aligned with our business?
- *Taking a Stand on Issues:* What issues make sense for our company to take a stand on? (If it's controversial, remember to assess your audiences and your risks.)

Natives vs. Immigrants   Many companies today are founded with a moral purpose that's core to their business strategy. An article in *Harvard Business Review* calls these types of brands "social purpose natives." The article states, "The societal benefit these 'social purpose natives' offer is so deeply entwined with the product or service that it's hard to see the brand surviving intact without it."[13]

Seventh Generation is a social purpose native that "made a promise the moment we named our brand." The company's mission is to inspire a consumer revolution that nurtures the health of the next seven generations. Its website articulates its beliefs about the rights of people and the planet, asserting that a company's values are as important as the products it makes. "We know that plant-based products can provide the efficacy you are looking for, and that products designed from renewable plant-based ingredients are a more sustainable option than ingredients made from petroleum. We believe that waste, is well . . . a waste. It's why we use recycled materials to design our packaging, and why we design our packaging to be recycled."

Kate Farms is another excellent example of a young company founded with powerful intentions of good . . . and a lot of heart. The company was formed by husband and wife team Richard and Michelle Laver to save their daughter Kate, who was born with cerebral palsy and was failing to thrive. It was founded on the belief that good nutrition leads to good health, and good health opens the door to endless possibilities. Today, the company offers a range of products offering functional nutrition for all ranges of dietary and medical needs.

Here's the company's story as told on its site:

> Kate Farms began with determined parents and a formula developed to save their young daughter, who was failing to thrive. This simple yet transformative idea of a formula that heals has grown into a family of medical nutrition formulas that help many discover new possibilities.
>
> Today doctors, dietitians, parents, caregivers, and those with medical and dietary needs are empowered with the choice of a new formula. It's nourishment that makes you feel good, because we all deserve nothing less.[14]

Salesforce.com is a standout example of a brand that began with a mission to do good for the world. It had a vision for a new kind of company with a new technology model, a new business model, and a new philanthropic model. Calling it the 1–1–1 model, it dedicates 1% of the company's equity, 1% of the company's product, and 1% of its employees' time to give back to communities throughout the globe. This innovative, integrated philanthropic model has been successful in its missions, giving more than $168 million in grants, 2.3 million hours of community service, and providing product donations for more than 32,000 nonprofits and higher education institutions.[15]Clearly, this is a deep value within the company founder, Marc Benioff, who has been pushing the tech industry to do more philanthropy. He and his wife Lynne have given more than $200 million to local children's hospitals.[16]

Of course, I have to mention Patagonia again here, as it is the quintessential example of a global brand built from the start to do good for the planet. TOMS, Warby Parker, and Gandys are other examples of companies created with a societal mission.

But what about existing companies that have been in operation without this key element of societal purpose? "Social purpose immigrants," as the *Harvard Business Review* article calls them.[17] Can these organizations effectively infuse this purpose into the very core of their organizations so that it becomes almost indigenous to the business? The answer is a resounding yes. Larger organizations across the globe are embracing this approach to business. I just mentioned a few above, but so many others— Unilever, SAS, Cisco Systems, Microsoft, Novartis, Toyota, GE, Deere—are among them.

Whether your company is a social purpose native or immigrant, one thing to note is that a moral purpose can and should evolve and expand over time. Many companies start with a single mission, but branch out to other related efforts. My advice is to remain true to your DNA and add efforts that are in sync with your original purpose. It can become a larger thematic with many initiatives under it, but make sure they fit together and make sense to your business and your constituents. This expansion will make your company rich with an even more powerful moral purpose, a stronger soul . . . and a stickier brand.

I spoke with Dianne Ledingham, partner and director at Bain & Company, about the new model. She shared her perspective on companies, older brands in particular, that are recognizing the importance of adapting to these new requirements:

> With the advent of technology, many old world companies are realizing they're going to be disrupted directly in their core business or in processes within their business because technology has disrupted every single core business process to some degree, as well as many industries. They know they're going to have to engage a different, more diversified workforce as they evolve their business model, even if their business isn't driven by millennials. To avoid disruption and engage their workforce, they recognize the need to focus on the dimensions in this new model. They are trying to determine what technology can do for their business strategy and what higher purpose they aspire to that will engage their employees and attract the kind of talent they need. They are looking at data to not only manage their service lifecycle, but also to find innovative ways to serve clients. So we're absolutely seeing companies raise these things in a way we haven't seen even as recently as seven to 10 years ago. And our business is evolving and responding to that.

Moral Purpose vs. Moral Code   I'm going to make a quick point here just to clarify moral purpose versus moral code. A *moral purpose* is one in which the company works to address world problems like hunger, racial/sexual inequality, climate issues like water shortages and fires, providing necessities like education, medicine, and homes to those in need or to underprivileged parts of the world, and offering access to information through things like no cost connectivity. As described in this chapter, this effort should be an act of good that is a natural extension of the business, part of a company's DNA. In and of itself, it is not designed to produce profit, but it delivers long-term value to an organization by bringing qualities to the brand that society demands, which ultimately makes an enterprise more valuable.

A company's *moral code* is a pledge to operate its business responsibly to minimize the harm it does to the planet. Recycling, reducing carbon footprint, and embracing other green practices that minimize energy and resource consumption are some efforts that fall into this category. This code will dictate how a company behaves in all aspects of its business, including how its products are developed and used, how the very nature of the business impacts the world, and how its management behaves in good times and in bad. This code is simply part of the new rules of engagement—requirements every company must deliver.

Wendy Miller, partner and chief marketing officer at Bain & Company, offered insights on how this moral code can deliver value across the board:

> We worked with one of the CPG companies helping them
> to reduce their packaging, which was a win, win, win.
> Consumers are happy that the company is doing better
> things for the planet and it's a lower cost for the company
> as well to reduce its packaging. It's good for the business.
> It's good for the world. It's good for the consumer.

Your Statement: Fuse Business Mission and Moral Purpose   Once the business strategy and moral purpose are clear, the next step is to create a statement that fuses these together, defining why a company exists and how it will positively impact the world. This simple statement will serve to clarify and anchor these critical missions.

Many businesses have separate company mission statements and moral purpose statements. I believe these two should be combined, as it demonstrates the tight integration between the two and illustrates what's truly at the core—within the soul—of the company.

Here are a few excellent examples:[18]

General Motors

To earn customers for life by building brands that inspire passion and loyalty through not only breakthrough technologies but also by serving and improving the communities in which we live and work around the world.

Pepsi

To deliver top-tier financial performance over the long term by integrating sustainability into our business strategy, leaving a positive imprint on society and the environment. We call this Performance with Purpose.

GE

To invent the next industrial era, to build, move, power and cure the world.

Patagonia

Build the best product, cause no unnecessary harm, use business to inspire and implement solutions to the environmental crisis.[19]

3. Be a Technology Company

Once a company has identified its business strategy and moral purpose, it should determine which technologies it will actively leverage (AI, apps, software, analytics, voice recognition, supply chain software, as examples) to deliver on both most effectively. This is another critical strategy, as using the right technology in the right way helps companies elevate their product/service offerings, improve their brand experience, and amplify their moral purpose.

In my last book, published in 2014, *The Digital Marketer*, George Colony, chairman and CEO of Forrester Research, said, "In the future, all companies will be software companies." I would argue that has already started to take hold. Forwarding-thinking organizations are leveraging technologies and applications that propel their companies forward by making their customers' lives better, easier, more fun . . . you name it. As Marc Andreessen said, "Software is eating the world." And it has. It now underlies and integrates everything. It is truly the pervasive enabler.

When I mention Colony's words to my clients, some are doubtful and apprehensive. These are typically companies in industries that are not technology driven. When this happens, I quickly alleviate their concerns. This doesn't mean they have to revamp their entire business model and start hiring programmers. What it does mean is that they must find and embrace those technologies that will enhance and evolve their businesses. I'm referring to technologies that streamline processes, solve problems, deliver a better customer experience, and help take brands to new places that can address world issues. This is something that every single company must do today, whether it is a smaller retailer serving a regional community or a global manufacturer of consumer goods that serves the entire world. The next generation of managers must understand the critical role software plays across all of its strategies, as it's paramount to success.

Some examples include Deere using software to help farmers maximize their crops; China-based Ant Financial's Ant Forest
tree-planting app, which is gamifying carbon footprint tracking
for more than 450 million users in China to help tackle climate
change[20]; and UNICEF's U-Report, a messaging platform that
engages young people in the political debate and carries out polls
on issues of importance to them. Answers are stored in a database and used to improve the work of UNICEF and its partners
in the field.[21]

4. Embrace Engagement Through Authentic Marketing

At this point in the process, a company should develop its engagement strategy, which is a better term for marketing communications because it more accurately reflects how this function has
evolved from a manipulative, interruptive, one-way, "talk at you"
process to a dialogue-driven dynamic in which a company lis-
tens and develops relationships, ultimately to establish trust and
deeper levels of engagement.

As these core components come together—a business strategy fueled by moral purpose, use of technology innovations to
elevate customer experience, and efforts to solve a problem in
the world—they provide great fodder for genuine, transparent,
and meaningful stories that can forge positive connections to
the brand.

Stories of a company's moral purpose, in particular, will be
the purest form of authentic marketing. When a company does
genuine good for the world, constituents will immediately recognize the authenticity in those stories, prompting them to like
and share them, and perhaps tell their own experiences with the
brand. This is the most powerful form of marketing a company
can experience, as it demonstrates how customers can serve to
co-create brands.

Those stories are just as critical to inspiring, motivating, and engaging employees. The Deloitte Global CMO explains the impact the network's WorldClass effort has on Deloitte's more than 260,000 people.

"Helping people connect to their purpose gives every aspect of their work more meaning," said O'Brien. "Our firms have committed their most valuable resources, their professionals, to help more than 50 million people around the world thrive; that is something so tangible, something we can all feel pride in for the impact we are making."

The next several chapters in this book (Part II) dive deeper into the "how" of authentic marketing, including the essential steps every marketer needs to master. It opens with a chapter on the history of marketing, which illustrates how this discipline has been gradually evolving from manipulation and interruption to authenticity, along the way shifting from transactional to relational interactions with customers. We'll cover the importance of constituency mapping, humanizing your brand, developing more authentic content, the role of data, and why earned media is reclaiming the lead in the paid, owned and earned equation.

Strategy Is Always On

Last, I want to make a point about the mindset everyone should embrace regarding a company's strategy. Far too many companies develop their business strategy and think, "Okay, we're done with this." Strategy is never done. It is a living, "always on" process that must continually adapt to our "always on" world. Changes in the political climate, shifts in market dynamics, emerging technologies, and evolving lifestyles/behaviors—all can impact your market, your customers, and your business. Companies must be fluid. This is essential to avoid disruption and obsolescence—and to remain relevant and prosperous.

As O'Brien eloquently put it: "There's no standing still. You simply cannot be complacent to it. You have to always be looking around the corner and know what the issues are today, what matters today, and everyone needs to be encouraged to see where they can take it next."

Notes

1. *New York Times*, Visionaries with the Courage to Change the World, May 24, 2018, www.nytimes.com/2018/05/24/us/visionaries-change-the-world.html

2. Deloitte 2018 Global Human Capital Trends, https://www2.deloitte.com/insights/us/en/focus/human-capital-trends.html

3. Deloitte 2018 Global Human Capital Trends, https://www2.deloitte.com/insights/us/en/focus/human-capital-trends.html

4. Mac Rumors, Apple Now Has 1.3 Billion Devices Worldwide, February, 1, 2018, www.macrumors.com/2018/02/01/apple-now-has-1-3-billion-active-devices-worldwide

5. *The Mercury News*, 1999: The Apple revolution—Jobs, Wozniak made technology attractive to the average consumer, August 29, 2014, www.mercurynews.com/2014/08/29/1999-the-apple-revolution-jobs-wozniak-made-technology-attractive-to-the-average-consumer

6. *Fortune*, Apple iPhone Owners: Here's How Many iPhones Are in Use, March 6, 2017, http://fortune.com/2017/03/06/apple-iphone-use-worldwide

7. Quora, www.quora.com/Did-Henry-Ford-actually-say-"If-I'd-asked-my-customers-what-they-wanted-they'd-have-said-a-faster-horse"

8. The Street, 5 Businesses That Missed Out Big Time, Dec. 6, 2011, www.thestreet.com/story/11332979/1/5-businesses-that-missed-out-big-time.html#5

9. Cone Communications CSR Study, www.conecomm.com/news-blog/2016-cone-communications-millennial-employee-engagement-study-press-release

10. Whirlpool, www.whirlpoolcorp.com/care-counts-school-laundry-program-exposes-link-between-clean-clothes-and-attendance

11. *Time*, These 10 Companies Are Changing the World, August 22, 2016, http://time.com/4461874/change-the-world-companies-fortune

12. *Time*, These 10 Companies Are Changing the World, August 22, 2016, http://time.com/4461874/change-the-world-companies-fortune

13. *Harvard Business Review*, Competing on Social Purpose, September–October 2017, https://hbr.org/2017/09/competing-on-social-purpose

14. KateFarms, www.katefarms.com/about

15. Salesforce.org, www.salesforce.org/pledge-1

16. SFGate, Benioff Donates Another $100 Million to Children's Hospitals, April 4, 2014, www.sfgate.com/health/article/Benioffs-donate-another -100-million-to-5384424.php

17. *Harvard Business Review*, Competing on Social Purpose, September–October 2017, https://hbr.org/2017/09/competing-on-social-purpose

18. Panmore Institute, http://panmore.com/?s=mission+statements

19. Patagonia, https://www.patagonia.com/home

20. *Fortune*, Change the World 2017, September 15, 2017

21. Social Tech Guide, www.socialtech.org.uk/projects/u-report

Authentic Marketing: Key Components

4

The Evolution of Marketing

Moving from Manipulation to Authenticity

With technology and humanity colliding and melding, it is creating an opportunity for marketing communications to reach its most evolved, most authentic form yet. We have been moving in this direction with the dramatic shifts created by digital communications, social media, and the Internet. Adding moral purpose to the equation has finally tipped the scales, enabling marketing to become more authentic and achieve what is considered to be the Holy Grail for brands—establishing trust and true engagement.

Before we get into the new rules of authentic marketing, let's take a quick look back at the evolution of marketing communications. This discipline, advertising in particular because that's how it all started, is most known for tactics of interruption and manipulation. It was creative and persuasive at best and contrived and deceptive at worst. Over the past few decades, innovations in business and technology have been gradually pushing marketing to a better place, changing it from company-centric and sales-driven to customer-centric and relationship-driven. Those major shifts have set the stage for moving from manipulation to a more authentic form of marketing.

Production Era

During this time (approximately 1860–1920), companies pushed products at people, believing that if they developed a quality product, it would sell itself. "If you build it, they will come" was the mindset in this industrial era. Businesses focused primarily on manufacturing; however, factories hadn't figured out mass

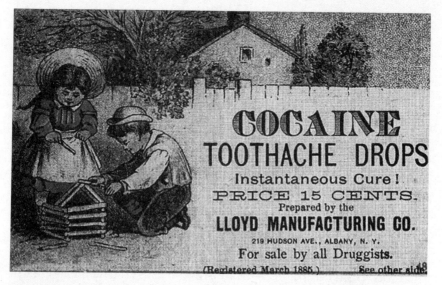

FIGURE 4.1 Ad to treat toothaches from 1885 in the Production Era
Source Dailymail.co.uk

production yet and products were scarce. Companies ignored the real needs of the market and did not adapt to customer needs. As such, marketing did not play a large role during this time period and was primarily in the form of print advertising and billboards.

The ad in Figure 4.1 is a classic example of the advertising approach used in this early era. Companies would often make outlandish claims touting drugs and products as miracle cures and could use a number of unimaginable and inappropriate tactics to sell products. The Cocaine Toothache Drops ad touted a product that was actually popular during the late 1800s to alleviate tooth pain in children. Back in those days, cocaine was considered a possibility for a local anesthesia and was often used to numb dental pain (it was later replaced by novocaine). It is believed that was the likely reason this company created a drop for children containing cocaine. In this ad, the drops promise an "instantaneous cure" to tooth pain.[1] It's an example of a "quack cure," using drugs in products and selling them as cures.[2] This ad illustrates the product-centric, one-way, push format that was used for decades.

FIGURE 4.2 Philip Morris ad from 1950s
Source reddit.com

Sales Era

After the industrial revolution, technological advances acceler-
ated product production, ushering in the Sales Era of marketing
(1920s–1940s). During the great depression, people bought
only the necessities and supply often exceeded demand. Competition was more intense. This drove companies to turn up
the volume on the hard sell, heavily using advertising to push
their products at people. Since products were not based on market need, companies had to convince customers to buy things.
Figure 4.2 is a classic ad from this era. Today it would be

unthinkable for a tobacco company to use a baby to sell cigarettes, but it was accepted back then. This ad was obviously created before we knew the hazards of cigarettes, but it still reflects how ads were designed purely to grab people's attention and push a product on them. The "sell" was that moms would never feel "over smoked" and that was the "miracle of Marlboro!" Again, this ad was designed to push a product on, in this case, women.

During this timeframe, marketing included print advertising and billboards, and expanded to radio. It was based on interruption and manipulation—interrupting what people were doing (reading or listening to the news or entertaining stories) to manipulate them into buying something.

Businesses continued to have a very myopic, company-centric view of the world. The customer was a one-size-fits-all, generic audience on the receiving end, having no power or voice. This established the one-way relationship between companies and customers.

Marketing Era

As consumers grew tired of the hard sell and having products forced on them, there was an evolution to the Marketing Era, beginning approximately in the mid-20th century, which is when the marketing department was born. This period was marked by a fundamental shift in focus: from the needs of the seller to those of the buyer. This change caused companies to start developing products that actually satisfied customer needs—what a novel idea! As an article in *AZCentral* put it, companies stopped "filling a hole in the factory" and started "filling a hole in the market."[3] Market research began playing a major role, helping companies identify products consumers actually wanted.

Broadcast advertising emerged as a core tactic, giving companies new ways to capture consumers' attention—and a new medium to interrupt and manipulate. However, this was often done creatively through likable characters like Tony the Tiger and Snap, Crackle, and Pop. Cult figures like the Marlboro Man also began to appear in campaigns.

Celebrity endorsements were also big, with actresses such as Farrah Fawcett and pop stars like Michael Jackson appearing in ads to sell everything from shampoo to cola. At the time, this strategy was designed to appeal to the masses, attempting to convince people to buy products simply because their favorite stars used them. While some of these ads were more creative and more entertaining, they all shared a common goal: persuade people to buy products.

The ad in Figure 4.3 features Farrah Fawcett, an iconic beauty, admired by men and women alike. Her feathered hairstyle has the distinction of being one of the 10 most requested hairstyles of all time, so having Farrah endorse a shampoo product

FIGURE 4.3   Farrah Fawcett promotes Wella Balsam shampoo in the 1970s
Source: Dazzling Divas Blog

was a natural fit.[4] After all, if Farrah loves Wella, why wouldn't you? The ad reflects how celebrity endorsements were used to influence purchasing decisions.

Relationship Marketing Era

Recognizing that acquiring new customers was more expensive than keeping current ones, marketers began to value the role of relationships and brand loyalty. Thus, the era of Relationship Marketing was born (mid-1990s–early 2000s). Companies began to focus more on efforts that built relationships with customers, with the hope of attaining their loyalty. Marketing relied less on mass media to persuade people to buy what they were trying to sell. Big data emerged as a means to help companies better understand audience segmentations. Direct marketing became a staple tactic as it attempted to reach and influence specific customer segments with messages showing a brand's relevance to them. It took the form of physical mail, email, and telemarketing, among other tactics. AOL was a massive user of direct marketing in the 1990s, distributing millions of computer discs that enabled people to go online if they had a modem. Stan Rapp, a pioneer in direct marketing, was a front-runner in this realm, building databases based on demographics for direct mail campaigns. One-to-one marketing, CRM, and data mining were the buzzwords of this era.

Digital Engagement Era

As the Internet and digital/social media started to become engrained in our culture, a seismic shift happened. As we moved into the 2000s, we entered the Digital Engagement Era, which ignited a massive power shift that put the reins directly in the hands of consumers, who now had the strongest and most important voice in the conversation. This is the single largest disruption marketing has experienced, bringing with it new channels with which to communicate, as well as a new paradigm with new rules.

Engagement was the prize all companies had their eyes on. The path to engagement involves listening to customers, having a dialogue with them, interacting with them where they live 24/7, serving up visual, bite-sized content that customers crave, and customizing content to fit individual needs. Telling versus selling—giving customers information that actually helps them versus simply manipulating and pushing a product on them— also remains key, as is the role of peer reviews. The art of storytelling emerged as a powerful way to engage, entertain, and enlighten audiences, showcasing lifestyles that represent the brand and meaningful stories that evoke emotions. Interruption techniques were diminished as new ad-free channels like Netflix emerged and options like ad blocking software, skip ad options, and paid ad-free subscriptions came on the scene.

We talked about media in terms of paid (ads, sponsored social media posts, underwriting, etc.), owned (websites, brochures, social media accounts, etc.), and earned (mentions/articles in the press, shares and engagement on social media, etc.), with some debate over which form of media served a company best. For a period of time, traditional media (the press) was undervalued in this equation, with paid and owned taking priority. You'll see in Chapter 9 how earned traditional media is once again ascending to the top spot, as other media (paid and owned) are playing more of a supporting role.

A number of technologies altered this landscape, such as the use of algorithms, which enable companies to customize information and actions to consumers. Google was the first to employ it to serve up customized ads and Amazon was out in front using

AI/machine learning to offer suggestions of books and other products. Netflix makes similar use of these technologies, suggesting shows based on programs you've watched.

Google, Facebook, and Amazon ushered in the era of data acquisition. This enabled us to move from using demographic to behavioral data, which provides far better insights into individual audiences. While many seem to be stuck on demographics, I believe it provides a simplistic and limited view of people—age, location, marital status, or income. Behavioral data, on the other hand, provides a clearer picture of who your customers are: what they like, what motivates them, how they spend their time, what keeps them up at night, etc. When used properly, this data helps marketers better understand and, therefore, better serve their customers, enhancing brand experience.

As exciting and enriching as this digital landscape is, it is also an incredibly complex environment to navigate. Businesses now must be always on, as nothing is ever complete and the world never shuts down. A tweet that has the potential to take down a brand can happen in the middle of the night. Opinions come at us from every corner, and we have to ascertain what's true and real and know how to distinguish the influencers from the noise. There are now endless distribution channels to follow, clicks to track, terabytes of data to sort, and sources of information to follow.

In addition, as companies are now in possession of a plethora of customer data, with that comes a huge responsibility to be an ethical keeper of that data to ensure it is used only for the public good. As Bing Song said in a recent *Washington Post* article, "Personal data once shared on platforms should no longer be viewed as the unencumbered private property of individuals or platforms. Instead, the data in circulation should be viewed as a public good, and data aggregators should become custodians of the public good."[5]

Enter Authentic Marketing

In spite of the complexities of this landscape, the Internet, digital media, and other technologies have without a doubt moved companies—and their marketing efforts—to a better place. It is now far more customer-centric, more personalized, more transparent, and less interruptive.

However, to thrive and truly engage in this elaborate environment, we need to continue to push marketing to its most evolved form yet—one of authentic marketing. The missing critical piece—moral purpose—holds the potential to propel us there by adding the key values and societal impact people crave and demand.

In this era, I believe marketing will become its best self—a more transparent, more genuine, more interesting, and less manipulative discipline. Companies must behave with more humanity, listening and responding to customers and operating every day with their values in mind. As their moral purpose comes to life, they should be sharing genuine, compelling stories about the ways they are working to positively impact people and the planet. Finally, companies should ensure their products do more good than harm.

They also need to use customer data honorably and with the right values, meaning for the good of the public and not for profit or manipulation. With businesses such as Amazon, Google, and Facebook providing so many streams of data to analyze, we will increasingly know more about consumers—their habits, lifestyles, likes, dislikes, etc. When this data is used for good, and I can't emphasize this enough, it can transform customers' experiences, making their lives richer, easier, safer, and more satisfying. To get there, we need to push on analytics to find those actionable elements that continue to evolve marketing to a better place, bringing better brand experiences to audiences and the world. This is how the use of big data must evolve to serve the greater good.

Companies taking this approach—operating with the right values, focusing on a meaningful moral purpose, and sharing compelling, genuine stories—are poised to capture the hearts and minds of customers. This is the essence of authentic marketing.

Patagonia's marketing director, Alex Weller, summed up the role of purpose in marketing well:

> You can't reverse into a mission and values through marketing. The organizations that are struggling with this are probably the ones that are thinking about marketing first. The role of marketing is to authentically elevate that mission and purpose and engage people in it, but the purpose needs to be the business.[6]

In this section of the book, you'll find the steps to deliver on this purpose. As with any evolution, you'll find some of them involve familiar skills, concepts, and approaches, but repurposed to infuse moral purpose and authenticity into your efforts. Others will, I hope, spark new thinking and new ideas, igniting new energy in your organization.

Notes

1. *Vintage Pharmacy Times*, Vintage Pharmacy Ad Promoted Cocaine Toothache Drops, December 17, 2014, www.pharmacytimes.com/careers -news/vintage-pharmacy-ad-promoted-cocaine-toothache-drops

2. *The Telegraph*, Cocaine Tooth Drops, Morphine Teething Syrup and Other Victorian Quack Cures, www.telegraph.co.uk/news/health/pictures /9519906/Cocaine-tooth-drops-morphine-teething-syrup-and -other-Victorian-quack-cures.html

3. *AZ Central*, What Are the Five Areas of Marketing, April 5, 2018, https:// yourbusiness.azcentral.com/five-eras-marketing-3411.html

4. *Total Beauty*, Farrah Fawcett, the 10 Most Requested Hairstyles of All Time, www.totalbeauty.com/content/gallery/most-requested-hairstyles /p63412/page3

5. *The Washington Post*, Big data as the next public good, May 2, 2018, www.washingtonpost.com/news/theworldpost/wp/2018/05/02/big -data/?noredirect=on&utm_term=.af6f754451b6

6. *Marketing Week*, Patagonia on why brands can't reverse into purpose through marketing, July 18, 2018, www.marketingweek.com/2018/07/18 /patagonia-you-cant-reverse-into-values-through-marketing/?ct_5b699 45ddbdee=5b69945ddbe90

Search for Truths to Drive Constituency Mapping

In a sense it's the new Marketing 101, viewed through the lens of your moral purpose. Companies need to know their audiences, and they need to know them well. Today, businesses have multiple constituencies they need to fully understand before mapping out communications strategies for each around their moral mission. In this way, every company should be searching for truths—truths about what their audiences care about, their passions, peeves, and opinions on controversial matters. In short, know what keeps them up at night and what gets them out of bed in the morning. Take their temperature and take it often.

This is critical as companies determine their moral purpose and make decisions about how to react to controversial issues that are relevant to their organization and stakeholders. When it comes to moral purpose—whether it's impacting climate change, helping to solve world hunger, upgrading education, protecting human rights, helping people in need, or addressing health issues—businesses need to understand how this aligns with the perspectives of their audiences. Even more importantly, when an organization decides to take action on more contested and controversial issues, such as gun control, immigration, LGBT rights, etc., it must have its finger on the pulse of constituents to understand how they'll react to this stance.

Building Your Data Toolbox

It wasn't all that long ago that the only ways we could get inside the minds of our customers was to conduct a telephone survey or focus group or have a good old-fashioned conversation with them.

Customer databases existed, but they provided only limited, static information. Technology has disrupted and transformed how we listen to and better understand our audiences. Tools such as social listening platforms, data analytics, first-generation marketing automation systems, customer relationship management systems, and cloud management platforms all hold the potential to bring enormous value to our efforts by giving us important and, in some cases, real-time insights into our customers.

These technologies will continue to expand and evolve, with new innovations becoming available that will be paramount to the success of our efforts. That's why it's critical that we as marketers continue to embrace new tools and technologies that enable us to better listen to, better understand, and ultimately better serve our customers across all our efforts and in our moral purpose initiatives specifically.

A Prospective View of Data

As the world continues to produce staggering amounts of data, new innovations will enable us to tap into it, extract meaning from it, and do it all in a timely manner to drive key decisions. To glean some insights into what's next for marketers in this realm, I spoke with Andy Frawley, CEO and vice chairman of the board of directors at V12 and former CEO of Epsilon. Here's his view:

It's a seminal issue and an unspoken digital reality that the magnitude of data that's being generated by our "always on" digital ecosystem is several orders of magnitude larger than the kind of customer database that we all lived and breathed by until fairly recently, say seven years ago.

There are three primary issues we need to address in this new landscape. First, there is a fundamental shift in how we should manage data. Today, we collect data, put it in a big warehouse or data lake, and manage it over a period of time. We must shift our thinking to acknowledge the new reality that data is constantly streaming in, and it's happening in real time. So from a data architecture standpoint, this notion of a streaming data environment is different than how we historically manage data. It's that always on mentality and an always on approach to managing data.

The second major trend that relates to this, particularly from a marketing standpoint, is the need to integrate the anonymous world with the authenticated world. The anonymous realm is one in which people search on the web without identifying themselves, and the authenticated realm is when someone is logged in and a brand knows exactly who that person is. Linking those two worlds together is something everyone seems to be working on right now. In many cases, the email address is the connective tissue between the authenticated and anonymous worlds, so many companies are trying to link cookies, device IDs, and various digital footprints with email addresses and physical addresses so first-, second-, and third-party data all come together. In this way, we are going to know people who have explicitly identified themselves, as well as people who haven't. That's the Holy Grail. Of course, all of this has an important sidebar around trust, privacy, and what's permissible. Ideally, we'll have pipes of streaming data and some type of canonical structure that enables you to identify what data can be used and in what circumstances.

The third big piece is where machine learning and AI kicks in—looking for signals that correlate to different data points—online, offline, authenticated, anonymous. The technology should be looking for signals within those streams of data that indicate there's something going on that needs further inspection or triggers some action. And that's where the real applications of machine learning come in. The system should inspect all of these signals and determine, for example, if Andy Frawley sleeps at 5 Elm Street five nights a week, that's probably his home address. Again, there are privacy issues that must be addressed with that, but it gives you the idea of how it would work.

Additional Tools and Technologies That Deliver Key Insights

There are also many tools that deliver insights into other key audiences, such as employees and influencers. For example, SurveyMonkey can help companies better understand their employees' perspectives on their moral purpose efforts, find out how it impacts employee perceptions of the company, and learn how it affects their job satisfaction and desire to stay at the organization. Another survey tool is a product called 15Five, which asks employees to take a 15-minute survey and then managers spend five minutes reviewing the answers. Pulse surveys are a fast and frequent survey system that asks simple questions often of employees to essentially take their pulse on key matters. Some systems like TINYPulse send out one simple question a week on various subjects through its app. These are just a few examples of how companies can readily secure employee feedback. Beyond these tools, questions around a company's purpose should always be part of employee reviews and ongoing conversations between management and employees.

There are also robust influencer technology tools and platforms, which leverage research and analytics to pinpoint and engage with top targets. These tools can provide precision in outreach, helping marketers find and build relationships with the most important influencers. These tools can be used to engage with the top-tier people who matter most, which maximizes the efficiency and impact of your outreach.

My advice to all marketers is to stay on top of tools and trends and be open to embracing them. All too often when

I discuss how technology and data are changing our industry, what I get in return is a little fear and a lot of avoidance. It's new, it involves change, and it's complex on some levels, so I get that. But in the end, I would advise people not to be so afraid of it or cling to the past. Move beyond focusing so much about what's under the hood and move toward understanding how these new tools can make your brand stronger, your connections deeper, and your organization more relevant.

An Inside Out Approach to Constituents

Let's move now to look at the various audiences and the critical role each of them plays in the effectiveness of your moral purpose. Start on the inside by building your base of champions among your employees and then work your way out to external audiences, such as customers, investors, watchdogs, and various influencers. Below we'll look at each audience in depth.

Employees

Employees are without a doubt the most critical audience on this list. It is only through their day-to-day contributions that a company can truly embed its moral purpose into its DNA and have a positive impact on the world.

Studies also show that employees are a company's "most believable" voice. Consumers say they believe about 16% of what companies tell them, but they believe a full 52% of what an employee says about a company.[1]

All of this underscores the importance of creating a culture of purpose—getting employees excited about and engaged in the process. The vast majority of people today, and millennials in particular, seek to work for purpose-driven organizations. They want to be part of something that's making a contribution to the planet.

A recent report by American Express found that among U.S. millennials, 68% want to be known for making a positive difference in the world; 81% said a successful business needs to have a genuine purpose that resonates with people; 78% want the values of their employer to match their own; and more than one-third define success as doing work that has a positive impact on society.[2]

This is the new criteria for attracting, motivating, and retaining top talent. To build a purpose-fueled culture, it must be woven into the fabric of the organization. Begin by sharing the vision and goals of your moral purpose. Explain how your company is going to make a meaningful, positive mark on the planet. Get people excited about those aspirations, the great work ahead, and the difference it can make. Involve employees in the effort at every step; they are integral to making it happen. Keep the effort alive through ongoing updates and acknowledge their work throughout the journey. Train and educate employees, as necessary, so they have the knowledge and skills to deliver on their part. Celebrate key milestones and other happenings to show momentum and build a strong sense of community around your mission. Use tools like SurveyMonkey to secure employee feedback on various aspects of your company's moral purpose. Last, reward employees for key contributions to reinforce what they are doing for the greater good. Chapter 10 goes deeper into how to build this type of culture of purpose.

Here are a few examples of how companies involve employees in their purpose:

Once again, Patagonia sets a great example. The company's goal was to "integrate innovative sustainability thinking, values, and goals into every employee by making sustainability the responsibility of *every* member of staff in *every* department of the business. By freeing corporate social responsibility from the confines of the CSR & sustainability department, Patagonia gets every employee involved in reducing the environmental footprint of the company."[3]

Among the company's many efforts is its employee activism program, which enables employees to get involved in a variety of interesting activities across the world. This includes its Environmental Internship Program in which employees from all parts of the company are allowed up to two months away from their regular roles to work for the environmental group of their choice while continuing to earn their paycheck and benefits.[4]

Below you'll find a few questions from a survey, found at questionpro.com, which highlights how a company like Patagonia works to secure important feedback from its employees about its core values.[5] This survey underscores how securing honest and valuable feedback from employees can help inform management on how the company is delivering on its key values. Feedback like this, as well as from external sources, can help inform key directions and decisions and keep a company in tune with its many audiences.

Patagonia Survey Participant

1. Product Quality: We strive to make the best products. The best products are responsibly made, durable, and multi-functional. They are perfectly suited to their end use. Product quality encompasses our commitment to the entire customer experience.

Well Above Expectations: We are viewed as the industry leader in product quality and innovation or, as one employee said, "We still deliver one new 'kick-ass' product after another!" We also maintain a seconds rate below 2% and remain an industry leader in advanced product initiatives.

Well Below Expectations: We are trying to appeal to too broad a range of people. We are "over" designing. Quality is suffering and customer complaints are rising.

(*continued*)

Patagonia Survey Participant (*continued*)

1 Well Above/Exceeds Expectations

2

3

4

5

6

7 Well Below Expectations

Comments/Suggestions on Product Quality:

_____

_____

2. Cause No Unnecessary Harm: We strive to reduce our environmental footprint. "Cause No Unnecessary Harm" means that we acknowledge that by being in business we cause some necessary harm. We continue to look for new ideas; some we try, some may fail, but we continue to make progress.

Well Above Expectations: We have numerous efforts underway to reduce our footprint; we share ideas across the organization; and we can quantify the reduction in our footprint.

Well Below Expectations: Our ideas are not getting traction; compared to prior years, we are losing momentum.

1 Well Above/Exceeds Expectations

2

3

4

5

6

7 Well Below Expectations

3. Environmental Activism: Three of our five tenets apply to this question—lead an examined life, support civil democracy, and influence other companies. "Clean up our own act" is addressed in Question 2 and 1% for the Planet is how we have chosen to distribute part of our profit. To lead an examined life is at the outset to be curious, to ask questions, and then to ask more questions. Civil democracy is the persistent and loud voice of the few changing the minds of others into results. To influence other companies is to lead by example.

Well Above Expectations: We create a climate that encourages environmental evangelism. We applaud the curious. We can cite ongoing or completed engagements of civil democracy. Other companies look to us as the example of the 21st century company.

Well Below Expectations: Our work environment discourages the curious thinker; our voice is becoming faint in civil democracy; we are undifferentiated from other companies in leading by example.

1 Well Above/Exceeds Expectations

2

3

4

5

6

7 Well Below Expectations

   Comments/Suggestions on Environmental Activism:

_____

_____

Source: https://www.questionpro.com/a/q/patagonia-2015–4200422

Another example is Cisco's initiative, which provides education, health care, economic empowerment, and disaster relief to areas in need. According to an article in *Hiring Success Journal*, the company's employees invest more than 160,000 volunteer hours globally in a year, working in teams called Civic Councils that organize events in their communities. Cisco asks its employees to *"be a part of the equation. You + Networks = Impact Multiplied."* [6]

At GE, "Ecomagination is one of the ways that employees find purpose in their work. Employees can engage in issues they are passionate about, either through their work with Ecomagination products that provide environmental benefits for customers or through helping GE meet its Ecomagination Greenhouse Gas (GHG) reduction and freshwater use goals."[7]

One Friday every month LinkedIn's employees participate in "InDay," giving back to the community through volunteerism and resources. InDay activities range from guest speakers discussing global justice to initiating global learning programs and volunteering in local communities.[8]

I interviewed two key people at Best Buy—Matt Furman, chief communications and public affairs officer, and Andrea Wood, head of social impact—to learn more about the many efforts the company has underway to deliver a higher purpose and to become a valuable member of the communities it serves. They talked about the important role that employees play in this mission.

"In retail, the best store general managers are the ones who are the most integrated into their communities and who train their staff to think of customers more as friends, relatives, and neighbors because your behavior changes when you think of them that way," said Matt Furman. "By definition, the word customer is run of the mill, but by definition, friends, neighbors, and family members represent something deeper, something richer. Our goal is to make that mindset the standard way in which we approach our customer base."

Andrea Wood added, "Our giving to local communities helps us show up as a community member, and not a nameless big box retailer. We bring Best Buy's unique assets and expertise to our programs. As an example, we are building teen tech centers to help teens from underserved communities prepare for the tech-reliant jobs of the future. We're expanding these centers with a plan to have more than 60 across the country by 2020. In addition, our community grants give our store managers the opportunity to make local funding decisions and foster closer relationships with nonprofits through funding as well as volunteering. Our stores are in the best position to know what their local communities need and how Best Buy can uniquely help."

Customers

Take off your marketing hat as we talk about this audience. To engage with customers, particularly when communicating stories about your moral purpose, you need to put traditional marketing tactics in the back seat . . . maybe even kick them to the curb. While marketing has evolved to become less manipulative and more genuine, many aspects of it remain designed and contrived. No matter how much we listen, have a dialogue, use visual mediums, and serve up desirable snackable content, many companies still approach customers with the sole purpose of selling them on a product, service or idea—those old "in-your-face" manipulation and interruption tactics.

An article in *Inc.* sums up this issue well:

It's not uncommon for brands to craft a compelling story and then dilute its effect by throwing a huge logo in the middle of it. Consumers rarely find this appealing, as they're attracted to authenticity. Try to resist making a story overtly about your brand. Instead, focus on producing a good story and let the word get out organically. Compare the effect of shouting to get a group's attention with speaking softly and forcing them to listen.[9]

By its very nature, your moral purpose is an ideal platform to tell genuine, transparent, and authentic stories. This type of content has all the elements of a compelling, engaging story that will speak to the humanity within us all, forging emotional connections with your audiences. Find creative ways to bring those stories to life across all of your channels and reveal what's inside the soul of your company. Incorporate content into websites, speeches, customer events, collateral, media outreach, and of course, on social media channels. When a company is doing genuine good for the world, those stories will sell themselves. More on effective storytelling can be found in Chapter 7.

Beyond telling stories, remember to listen closely to this audience. As mentioned earlier in this chapter, use all of the listening and analytics tools at your disposal to make sure you know your customers well—their passions and their peeves. Gain insights into their views about your moral purpose and other pressing issues to ensure your efforts are in sync with their values and concerns.

Know particular audience segments inside and out in terms of where and how to reach and listen to them in the social sphere. Here are some social media usage stats from early 2018 compiled by Pew Research Center. The majority of Americans across a wide range of demographics use Facebook, but YouTube is now used by nearly three-quarters of U.S. adults and 94% of 18 to 24 year olds. Moreover, young adults (18 to 24) are particularly heavy users of Snapchat (78%), Instagram (71%), and Twitter (45%). However, other platforms appeal more strongly to select subsets of the population. For example, Pinterest is more popular among women than men. LinkedIn is particularly popular among college students and high-income households. WhatsApp is popular in Latin America and also Latinos living in the United States.[10]

Facts like these, along with in-depth knowledge of your particular customer segments, will help you understand how to meet your audiences where they live. Keep pace with the changing use of social channels as their place in our society continues to evolve.

Invite customers into your efforts to change the world, essentially helping to transform them into ambassadors for your mission. Let customers know how they can make a donation, welcome their participation in events for a specific cause (whether it's cleaning up a community or embarking on a humanitarian trip), or just ask them to share their stories about a particular issue the company is working to address.

TOMS has accomplished this through its One Day Without Shoes (ODWS) initiative. Every year in May, TOMS asks its digital community, the TOMS Tribe, to post a picture of their bare feet on Instagram with the hashtag #WithoutShoes. For every post, the brand donates a pair of shoes to a child in need. According to an article in *MarketingWeek*, the event engaged 3.5 million people in one day.[11]

My last point about customers goes back to broader company values and priorities. Every move you make should go back to this one critical question: "Is this good for my customers?" Ask this question across every aspect of your organization, whether you are developing new products/services, creating new systems and processes, implementing new technologies, or deciding how to use their data. It should be the filter everything flows through.

Investors

While this audience may care about the good your company is doing for mankind (at a minimum, it has their attention since Laurence Fink's letter), what matters most is understanding how these efforts are going to deliver value to your bottom line. For this audience, you need to explain how your moral mission will provide a competitive advantage and deliver improved financial performance. In the profit meets purpose equation, it's about demonstrating how purpose will deliver profit. This involves articulating how it will deliver long-term value (versus short-term/quarterly profitability), showing how your purpose helps attract top talent, builds a strong, relevant brand, creates meaningful shareholder engagement, and how it is tied to your company's overall business mission.

Proof of Purpose Driving Profit

The connection between purpose and profit is nicely articulated by a study from Deloitte. The company compiled research on social value creation and found at least six ways purpose delivers quantifiable business benefits.

> Our research provides evidence of six key drivers of social value creation, beyond rhetoric and sentiment, to support champions of corporate social strategy and help persuade skeptics that companies can do well by doing good.[12]

Key findings from Deloitte's research include:

1. Mitigating regulatory risks and securing a social license to operate are long-standing motivators for companies to adopt a social strategy but are increasingly mere table stakes in today's competitive landscape.[13]
2. The majority of consumers say they will pay more for products from socially responsible companies—and consumers are increasingly following through on their convictions. Brands with a demonstrated commitment to sustainability are seeing average sales growth outperform brands without demonstrated commitment by fourfold.[14]

3. Identifying underserved social and environmental needs are strong drivers of innovation, enabling companies to explore new models and technologies that generate new market opportunities.[15]

4. Companies with a strong social strategy tend to see higher employee engagement, and "high engagement" companies have been found to significantly outperform "low engagement" companies in year-over-year changes in net income and stock earnings per share.[16]

5. Operational efficiencies from more sustainable practices can save companies up to 45% in costs, with an ever-growing list of major companies seeing annual savings in the hundreds of millions.[17]

6. Capital markets tend to reward socially active firms, with companies added to the Domini 400 Social Index realizing a 2% gain in share price on average, while those removed from the list saw a 3% loss.[18]

Corporate Watchdogs

Government organizations, industry associations, nonprofits, and other activists play a critical role in policing companies to make sure they do no harm and tell no lies. These organizations call out companies who make false claims and promises. The Federal Trade Commission (FTC), for example, has a series of truth in advertising standards that companies must abide by. Skechers is among the many companies that violated those standards, claiming its shoes could help customers get in good shape and improve their cardiovascular health.[19] The Food and Drug Administration (FDA) has also taken action against a number of products causing harm, such as Hydroxycut for causing health issues.[20] Consumer activists also have brought suits to companies with false claims, such as the mother who sued Nutella for touting its chocolaty, nutty spread as a healthy breakfast option.[21]

Organizations such as the FTC and the FDA provide value in ensuring companies deliver on their promises and do no harm. Companies must communicate with them regularly, providing facts and reports that demonstrate the progress being made on societal missions such as sustainability. It also means never making false claims and validating claims with scientific facts.

Media

It wasn't all that long ago we heard the dire predictions of how digital would kill traditional media, with newspapers, broadcast news, and magazines going the way of modems, pagers, and typewriters. Not only did that never come to pass, but traditional, respected media outlets have a renewed importance in our society. Sure, digital technology caused a massive disruption to media, forcing news sources to embrace new mediums, new distribution channels, new formats, and new ways of listening to and interacting with readers. However, trusted, credible media—reshaped in new multi-media, visual, and interactive formats—are among the most critical sources of information. This is particularly true as we struggle to navigate through an ever-rising sea of information, maneuvering to dodge "fake news" and avert highly biased sources with focused agendas.

As this form of earned media rises to reclaim its lead in the paid, owned, and earned equation, it is more important than ever for companies to know their top media targets. I'm talking about the top 10 to 20 reporters who truly have an influence on your audience and market. Once you've identified this audience, you need to get a sense of their interest level relating to your company's societal purpose. Do some digging to see how they cover subjects like sustainability and other forms of corporate good.

In this process, you may discover new influencers who follow and cover these topics. Make it your business to start building relationships with them and then serve up the kind of content that interests them most. For more on the growing importance of earned media, see Chapter 9.

Other Influencers

When the Internet leveled the playing field, it created a new base of influencers . . . and they could exist in any corner of the world. This new category of influencers might include a prominent You-Tuber living in New York City or a respected blogger living in Barrow, Alaska. Find the influencers who matter most to your audiences and ensure you are communicating with them regularly.

Analysts

For markets with industry analysts (like technology, health care, or insurance), it's critical to inform these audiences of your moral purpose and keep them apprised of how you are doing against this mission. Companies like Forrester Research, Altimeter, and Gartner, as examples, often track and write reports on these types of initiatives, so continue to keep them apprised. As moral purpose evolves to become a core business strategy, my hope is that research firms will increasingly measure and report on the impact these efforts are having on businesses, industries, and the world.

The most important point I'd like people to take away from this chapter is to embrace new technologies, tools, and processes that hold the power to deliver critical insights into all of your audiences. Use everything at your disposal to listen to and understand each audience segment so that your efforts are in sync with them and to glean feedback that can steer the direction of your moral purpose. The world of data is exploding, and we are making great strides in harnessing it. Use that data—with the right ethics and the best intentions always—to better understand audiences, to deliver more authentic communications, and to guide your moral purpose.

Notes

1. Sustainable Brands, Employees Are Your Best Purpose Ambassadors, March 2, 2018, www.sustainablebrands.com/news_and_views/marketing_comms/dr_john_izzo/employees_are_your_best_purpose_ambassadors

2. American Express Survey, November 29, 2017, *Redefining the C-Suite: Business the Millennial Way*, http://about.americanexpress.com/news/pr/2017/millennials-plan-to-redefine-csuite-says-amex-survey.aspx

3. CSRCentral, March 4, 2015, Patagonia—The Clothing Company with a Revolutionary Approach to CSR and Sustainability, http://csrcentral.com/patagonia-the-clothing-company-with-a-revolutionary-approach-to-csr-sustainability

4. Patagonia Environmental Internship Program, www.patagonia.com/environmental-internship-program.html

5. Patagonia 2015, www.questionpro.com/a/q/patagonia-2015-4200422

6. *Hiring Success Journal*, January 16, 2018, Lexie-Forman-Ortiz, Top 10 Corporate Social Responsibility Efforts, www.smartrecruiters.com/blog/top-10-corporate-social-responsibility-initiatives

7. General Electric, Ecomagination, www.gesustainability.com/building-things-that-matter/energy-and-climate/employee-engagement

8. *Hiring Success Journal*, Lexie-Forman-Ortiz, Top 10 Corporate Social Responsibility Efforts, January 16, 2018, www.smartrecruiters.com/blog/top-10-corporate-social-responsibility-initiatives

9. *Inc.*, Three Ways to Use Storytelling to Attract Your Audience, www.inc.com/jeremy-goldman/3-ways-to-use-storytelling-to-attract-your-audience.html

10. Pew Research Center, Social Media Use in 2018, March 1, 2018, www.pewinternet.org/2018/03/01/social-media-use-in-2018

11. *MarketingWeek*, How TOMS Engaged 3.5 Million People in One Day, June 29, 2016, www.marketingweek.com/2016/06/29/how-footwear-brand-toms-engaged-3-5-million-people-in-one-day-using-tribe-power

12. Deloitte, Perspectives, Social Purpose and Value Creation, https://www2.deloitte.com/us/en/pages/operations/articles/social-value-creation.html

13. Deloitte, Perspectives, Social Purpose and Value Creation, https://www2.deloitte.com/us/en/pages/operations/articles/social-value-creation.html

14. The Deloitte Consumer Review, "The Growing Power of Consumers," 2014.

15. Deloitte, Perspectives, Social Purpose and Value Creation, https://www2 .deloitte.com/us/en/pages/operations/articles/social-value-creation.html

16. Cone Communications, "2015 Cone Communications / Ebiquity Global CSR Study," 2015.

17. Nielson, "Sustainable Selections: How Socially Responsible Companies Are Turning a Profit," October 12, 2015.

18. Towers Perrin, "Employee Engagement Underpins Business Transformation," 2009.

19. Federal Trade Commission website, Skechers Will Pay $40 Million to Settle FTC Charges That It Deceived Customers with Ads for Toning Shoes, www.ftc.gov/news-events/press-releases/2012/05/skechers-will -pay-40-million-settle-ftc-charges-it-deceived

20. CNN, Stop Using Hydroxycut products, FDA Says, CNN.com, May 1, 2009, www.cnn.com/2009/HEALTH/05/01/hydroxycut.fda.recall /index.html

21. *Parenting*, Moms Wins Class Action Suit Over Nutella's Misleading Ads, www.parenting.com/blogs/show-and-tell/caitlin-parentingcom/ mom-wins-class-action-suit-over-nutellas-misleading-ads-0

CHAPTER
6

Humanize Your Brand

To be truly authentic, one essential element that *underlies everything* is making your brand more human and operating with more humanity. If you are genuine and good at the core, it will flow through every aspect of your business and reveal itself in everything you do. Be aware that you can't silo authenticity to your moral purpose efforts, only to behave differently in other aspects of your business.

Humanizing your brand involves taking on character traits customers value most in their relationships with other people. Qualities like honesty, empathy, openness, and being respectful are among the behaviors companies should embrace. This process will make your brand more real, more relatable, more likeable, and more authentic. Most importantly, displaying the right human qualities help consumers *feel* a connectedness to your brand. This elevates your company from one that people can simply buy products from (transactional) to one they also admire, respect, relate to, like . . . maybe even love (relational). The difference in this equation is the emotional connection, and it's huge.

Generally speaking, businesses have been built to be *anything but* human. We talk in corporate speak, rely on numbers to tell stories, strip emotions out of the dialogue, essentially operate like a machine. I'll reference back to the words of Mark Fuller, chairman of Rose Global and co-founder of Monitor Group (now Deloitte Monitor): "We can comfortably talk numbers, but not about all those embarrassing issues where you might have to use words like love, or change the world, or have deep meaningfulness to what you do. It's not businesslike."

However, there's growing evidence that acting more human is directly linked to company performance. According to a report from C Space, "CQ17: Unlocking Customer Inspired Growth," based on three years' worth of data from nearly 65,000 consumers in the U.S. and UK provides "compelling evidence that businesses that act more human outperform those that don't. The companies that outperform their competitors have learned to act more like their customers—to take on human qualities in their actions . . . . These leading companies have become more customer centric by acting more human."[1]

So how exactly does a business act more human? Start the effort by making an objective assessment of your organization's overall customer experience, looking not only for strengths, but particularly for areas that fall short. From an operations perspective, does your organization have the right processes, tools, and technology to deliver a more human (more relational, less transactional) experience? Are your employees equipped to deliver this new level of customer care? In other words, are they free to make decisions that can solve customer problems and also delight them? From a values perspective, does your organization operate day to day in a way your customers feel good about, relate to, and admire? From a communications perspective, are you interacting with an approach that builds trust, forges connections, and garners respect? The answers you receive to these questions will help guide where you need to focus.

To gain an outside perspective on these matters, C Space suggests involving customers in the process: "Get to know some personally, invite them into your facilities and meetings, run ideation and co-creation sessions with them, give them ongoing forums for feedback and suggestions, bring them to life as complex, quirky individuals in your hallways, cafeterias, and boardrooms . . . . Develop the daily practice of putting yourself in their shoes."[2] By doing so, companies can become more customer-centric, which is the pathway to acting more human.

Use Technology to Show Your Human Side

While it may seem counterintuitive, one way of acting more human involves using technology. Today we're mired in too many conversations about technology. We need to move beyond that and figure out how to use technology to better understand our customers, to delight them, and to create connections that show the human side of our brand. A quick example of this is how Amazon uses machine learning to offer suggestions on books and other items while you are shopping on its site. This personalized experience makes the shopper feel like someone on the other end is helping out with suggestions based on their shopping preferences. Starbucks' use of crowdsourcing technology offers another example. The company's My Starbucks Idea invited customers to submit new ideas and suggestions to the company. This made customers feel like company insiders and enabled them to be a key part of changes and improvements at Starbucks. The technology helped Starbucks not only tap directly into customer needs and ideas, but also to show its human side and remain relevant through technology and data.[3]

Achieve Deeper Engagement

Bringing out the human side of your brand can forge stronger and deeper connections with customers. Let's drill down into specific marketing/engagement efforts that can make your brand more human and your outreach more authentic.

Put Honesty First

Trust is in a state of crisis right now in the United States, according to Edelman's 2018 Trust Barometer. Among the reasons are an enormous lack of faith in the government, as well as distrust in media (primarily search engines and social media), with the majority of respondents saying they have trouble identifying good journalism from falsehoods.[4]

Because of this, building trust should be the number one job for companies and their CEOs. This means that communicating openly and honestly (and quickly when there's an issue or a crisis) is paramount. It also means being fully transparent about your products and services. Studies show that 94% of consumers are likely to be loyal to a brand that offers complete transparency.[5] That's a big number; proving this should be a big priority.

Southwest Airlines' much talked about "Transfarency" campaign is a great example of how this can be put into action. The low-cost, nonconformist airline made a pledge to treat customers honestly and fairly with low fares that stay low with no hidden fees or extra costs. Combining this with the hashtag, #FeesDontFly, the airline highlighted its value proposition, differentiated itself from the pack, and earned the trust and loyalty of customers. Figure 6.1 shows Southwest Airline's Transfarency Tweet from this highly successful campaign. The no-frills airway also generated nearly five million likes on Facebook with this campaign.[6]

General Motors (also highlighted in Chapter 3) demonstrates how the company took an honest internal assessment of itself and its "unintended negative consequences" of crashes, emissions, and congestion, which ultimately provided a powerful and meaningful foundation for its moral purpose. "As we looked through an authentic lens of feedback loops from our audiences and tried to understand not just the good we provide, but also the negative outcomes, we boiled it down to the need to create a safer, simpler, better solution. This was the foundation for our idea of zero crashes, zero emissions, zero congestion," said Tony Cervone, General Motors' senior vice president of global communications. Cervone added that,

Southwest Airlines ✔ @SouthwestAir · 8 Oct 2015
Halftime. For everyone except Transfarency. #AlwaysOn #FeesDontFly
transfarency.com

💬 13   🔁 46   ♡ 82   ✉

FIGURE 6.1 Southwest Airlines' Transfarency tweet
Source Southwest Airlines

although those negative consequences were completely unintended, the company felt a strong responsibility to work toward solutions to them. This honest approach enabled GM to discover this important purpose.

Infuse Empathy in Your Culture

Empathy is another absolutely essential trait that must be infused throughout an organization—a cultural criteria for success. Listening to and understanding others can forge stronger connections and foster necessary changes inside an organization. As an article in *Harvard Business Review* put it, empathy "is more important to a successful business than it has ever been, correlating to growth, productivity, and earnings per employee."[7] There's even an Empathy Index, which takes a scientific approach to measuring empathy inside corporations.[8]

Deloitte Global CMO Diana O'Brien explains the importance of empathy in Deloitte's culture: "Empathy is a huge part
of making an impact that matters because unless you can understand what really matters to a client it's hard to make an impact.
And you don't really understand what matters unless you have
empathy. We have even developed a course to help our people
hone their empathic skills, it's that important to us."

Stand Out by Standing Up

Companies today are expected to take a stand on issues and demonstrate they are working to solve societal problems. A study by
Sprout Social found that approximately two-thirds of consumers
said it was either somewhat or very important for brands to take
a stand on social/political issues.[9]

Today, an increasingly number of corporations are no longer looking the other way and are instead staring issues squarely
in the eye, taking them head on. For example, Salesforce's Marc
Benioff took a stand against North Carolina's transgender
"bathroom law"[10] and Amazon's Jeff Bezos opposed an executive
order that banned refugees and visa holders from seven majority Muslim countries from traveling to the United States.[11] In
the wake of the Parkland, Florida, shooting, several big brands
(Delta, Avis, Budget, and Symantec among them) cut their ties
to the NRA.[12]

One creative example of this is when Patagonia confronted
our society's over-consumption habits and their impact on the
planet through its Black Friday "Don't Buy This Jacket" campaign, which started in 2011 (Figure 6.2). The company issued
a call to action to make people think twice before purchasing
a new jacket because of the resources required to make it. The
company instead urged people to repair, recycle, or simply wear
something old instead of buying something new—powerful stuff

FIGURE 6.2   Patagonia's Don't Buy This Jacket Black Friday ad
Source Target Marketing

and completely counter to what businesses and Black Friday are all about. This revealed and reinforced Patagonia's deep values of doing right by our planet. In 2016, the company continued the ad, but announced it would give away 100% of its global retail and online profits from Black Friday to nonprofits working to protect the environment. Through this effort, Patagonia donated $10 million in sales[13] . . . talk about putting your money where your mouth is!

Be Provocative

Being provocative is a personality trait that has served a number of brands well, helping them to stand out in the market with messages that not only catch people's attention, but resonate with their values and ideals. T-Mobile exemplifies the amazing impact this approach can have when done right.

T-Mobile is a company with a strong counterculture personality. It's projected through the big, outspoken, and passionate personality of the company's CEO John Legere, who breaks

FIGURE 6.3   T-Mobile's provocative ad
Source https://socialhospitality.com/2014/10/can-learn-t-mobiles
-social-strategy

new ground by breaking the rules. Through the company's "Un-carrier" movement and its unconventional leader who calls out competitors as "dumb and dumber," T-Mobile set out to drastically change the carrier model, offering customers something no one else in the industry did: no contracts, no subsidized phones, no coverage fees for data, and no early termination fees. Along the way, he redefined the wireless industry.

The Un-leash, Don't Play by Rules, Break Them ad (Figure 6.3) highlights T-Mobile's provocative and effective approach. Taking the competition head on, the ad states: "Other wireless carriers just can't let go of their lame rules. They say that's the way it is. We say, not cool." The ad then bullets the company's rule-breaking benefits like no upgrade runarounds, no annual service contracts, etc.

This approach has paid off, with T-Mobile winning the hearts, minds, business, and loyalty of customers (the company added five million new customers in 2017)[14] and securing the spot as the third largest and fastest growing wireless carrier in the United States.[15]

Reveal Your Personality

When you truly know your customer base, you understand the kind of personality they'll relate with and be attracted to. Your brand should project that persona, enabling your customers to create a connection with your company as they would with another person. Think about the kind of person your brand should emulate. Are you an earthy, outdoorsy brand? A savvy, urban brand? A funny, self-deprecating brand? A tech-savvy, forward-thinking brand? A compassionate brand that champions the underdog? What character traits go along with that? What lifestyle? What values? Once you determine who you are, this will guide your voice, your tone, your words, and your actions. It will help you to know what you stand for . . . and when you should stand up for something your customers are passionate about.

Here's a great example:

While there are scores of companies selling water bottles, Hydroflask stands out as a brand with a great product and a magnetic personality that is all about living a fun, active, and adventurous life. Figure 6.4 brings all of that to life. A quick look at the image and you get a strong sense of the brand's personality . . . and of the kind of people who buy the product. This photo also puts people over product, making it more relatable and more human. Another strong benefit is that for each purchase you make, the company gives back 5% of the proceeds to one of their 12 charities or nonprofit partners.[16]

FIGURE 6.4   Hydroflask fun and adventurous photo
Source http://pages.prime-incororated.com/blog/5-companies
-with-a-magnetic-personality

This website copy brings to life the personality of the brand and the lifestyle of its customers:

> We'll keep water icy cold on a hot sunny beach. And serve up a hot coffee on the chairlift ride. We'll sit patiently by your camp chair with frosty cold beer while you gather wood for the fire. Or keep you hydrated on a hike: ice, water, go. And five hours later, after driving to the trailhead and climbing 2,000 feet, you'll still have ice and water while you enjoy the view. We'll bring you hot tea on misty riverside mornings when the steelhead are running, hot cocoa to coax your kids along a snowy trail, and a refreshing sip of "all-about-you" during Saturday afternoon yoga. We're not just along for the ride. We're along to help make the ride awesome.[17]

Paint the Faces of Your Brand

Putting some of the key faces in your company front and center is a powerful way to reveal the human side of your organization. Map those faces to the strategy model outlined in Chapter 3, with key people becoming of the voices of business, moral purpose, technology, and engagement content:

- The CEO should be the lead voice of the business strategy and moral purpose, articulating the vision and the strategy and serving as the most passionate champion of the good the company seeks to do in the world.
- The CIO should be the face of how the company is using technology for the good of customers, with the right moral code and values to amplify its moral mission.
- The CMO or VP of Marketing should champion and articulate engagement to show how the company is implementing authentic marketing strategies to have a better dialogue, to listen more closely, to share more compelling content, and to ensure society's call for company values and action are being met.

Say You're Sorry

Humanizing your brand also means you need to own up to problems, apologize for them . . . and do it fast. I can't stress this enough. Hiding in silence or, worse yet, getting defensive when something is clearly wrong is a massive mistake that will cost you on multiple levels. In today's world, in which everyone with a cell phone can videotape an event, company behavior gone bad can go viral in a flash. And people love seeing the bad guys get caught. Companies need to be prepared to own issues, say they're sorry for them, accept responsibility, acknowledge the victims, and show how they're going to fix things. These are desirable human traits that earn trust and respect. You'll be surprised at how forgiving people will be when you deal with difficult situations with honesty, transparency, integrity, and a little humble pie . . . all of the traits you'd want in a good friend.

PwC Apology for Academy Awards Error   PricewaterhouseCoopers gave an award-winning apology when the Academy Awards announced the wrong winner for best film because the announcers had been given the wrong category envelope. Here's the statement:

> We sincerely apologize to *Moonlight*, *La La Land*, Warren Beatty, Faye Dunaway, and Oscar viewers for the error that was made during the award announcement for Best Picture. The presenters had mistakenly been given the wrong category envelope and, when discovered, was immediately corrected. We are currently investigating how this could have happened, and deeply regret that this occurred. We appreciate the grace with which the nominees, the Academy, ABC, and Jimmy Kimmel handled the situation.[18]

Taylor Swift Makes Apple Do a U-Turn   Showing strong disapproval of Apple's new policy of not paying artists' royalties on its new streaming service, Taylor Swift announced on Tumblr she would be withholding her platinum-selling 1989 album from the new subscription service. True to her style of not being afraid to stand up for the rights of others, Taylor implored the "astronomically successful Apple" to pay "artists less fortunate than her." Within 24 hours, in a series of Tweets, Apple did a complete about-face and changed its policies.[19] In a series of Tweets, Eddy Cue of Apple stated:

> "Apple will always make sure artist are paid #iTunes #AppleMusic"
> "#AppleMusic will pay artist for streaming, even during customer's free trial period"
> "We hear you @taylorswift#13 and indie artists. Love, Apple."

Now that's a "swift" apology.

Ditch the Corporate Speak

Talk corporate to me . . . said no one ever. This is one of the fastest ways to lose your audience. Not only do people not relate to it, but they don't trust it and tune out as soon as they hear it. It sounds—and is—contrived language that is inauthentic. Use plain language. Talk to your customers as if you were talking to a friend.

The words of IBM former CEO Thomas Watson, Jr. sum this plain and simple:

> Gobbledygook . . . may be acceptable among bureaucrats but not in this company. IBM was built with clear thinking and plain talk. Let's keep it that way.[20]

Words to live by.

Show Your Funny Bone

Nothing is more endearing to people than giving them a good belly laugh. So don't be afraid to show your lighter side. Charmin's play on words of streaming while streaming is a great example of infusing humor in social media outreach. Making

FIGURE 6.5 Charmin shows its lighter side on Twitter
Sources https://blog.hubspot.com/marketing/funny-brands-social-media; https://twitter.com/Charmin

people laugh is an engaging way to bring forth the human side of your brand. It also makes people feel that the company doesn't take itself too seriously. These traits are appealing and create positive associations with the brand. Some companies base their entire campaigns on humor to get people hooked on watching their ads or following tweets.[21]

And Jetblue made us smile with its #snowmandatingproblems hashtag and tweet. As a Hubspot blog noted, the company "sprinkles in just a little humor throughout its social presence ... balancing informational content with lighthearted updates like the post below."[22] When a company takes this approach, it provides the information customers need and also reveals the lighter, human side of the brand, which can forge an emotional connection. It drives home the quote, "Laughter is the closest distance between two people."[23]

FIGURE 6.6 JetBlue's tweet makes us smile
Source JetBlue

Showing the human side of your company is key to being more authentic. By revealing a more real, more personal side of your company, it makes your brand more relatable, more likeable, and more genuine. Ultimately, this can help build trust and forge new levels of engagement that can create deeper, more emotional connections to your brand.

Notes

1. C Space Report, CQ17: Unlocking Customer Inspired Growth
2. C Space Report, CQ17: Unlocking Customer Inspired Growth
3. Business2Community, 6 Forgotten Ways Technology Makes Your Brand More Human, www.business2community.com/marketing/6-forgotten -ways-technology-makes-brand-human-01577784
4. 2018 Edelman Trust Barometer, www.edelman.com/news-awards/2018 -edelman-trust-barometer-reveals-record-breaking-drop-trust-in-the-us

5. Label Insight, 2016 Transparency ROI Study, www.labelinsight.com /Transparency-ROI-Study

6. Visioncritical, 5 Brands that Employed Transparency in Marketing and Won, July 8, 2016, www.visioncritical.com/5-brands-employed -transparency-marketing-and-won

7. *Harvard Business Review*, The Most Empathetic Companies, 2016, https:// hbr.org/2016/12/the-most-and-least-empathetic-companies-2016

8. The Empathy Business, http://theempathybusiness.co.uk/empathy-brand -index

9. *AdWeek*, Major of Consumers Want Brands to Take a Stand on Social and Political Issues, January 12, 2018, www.adweek.com/brand-marketing /majority-of-consumers-want-brands-to-take-a-stand-on-social-and -political-issues-according-to-new-study

10. *CBS News*, Salesforce CEO: Speaking Out on Social Issues is the "right thing to do," June 1, 2016, www.cbsnews.com/news/salesforce-ceo-marc-benioff -north-carolina-bathroom-law-artificial-intelligence-future-of-tech

11. *Forbes*, Jeff Bezos Opposes Immigration Order as Amazon Supports Washington AG Suit Against Trump, January 30, 2017, www.forbes.com /sites/ryanmac/2017/01/30/amazons-jeff-bezos-issues-strong-statement -opposing-trumps-immigration-order/#76c1a10261b6

12. *The Independent*, Here are all the brands that have cut ties with the NRA following gun-control activists' boycotts, February 25, 2018, www .independent.co.uk/news/world/americas/nra-florida-shooting-gun -control-national-rifle-association-arming-teachers-donald-trump -latest-a8227836.html

13. Patagonia, www.patagonia.com/blog/2016/11/record-breaking-black -friday-sales-to-benefit-the-planet

14. T-Mobile Newsroom, https://newsroom.t-mobile.com/news-and-blogs /q4-customers.htm

15. *Business Insider*, Oct 7, 2016, http://www.businessinsider.com/t-mobile -ceo-john-legere-interview-2016–10

16. Prime, The Awesome Sauce Marketing Blog, July 8, 2016, http:// pages.prime-incorporated.com/blog/5-companies-with-a-magnetic -personality

17. Hydroflask, www.hydroflask.com/explore/our-story

18. Glean.info, 5 Examples of Superb Company Apologies, March 22, 2017, https://glean.info/5-examples-superb-company-apologies

19. *Washington Post*, Taylor Swift Just Took on Apple and Won, June 22, 2015, www.washingtonpost.com/news/morning-mix/wp/2015/06/22 /taylor-swift-just-took-on-apple-and-won/?noredirect=on&utm_term= .e684435f3605

20. Communico, Gobbledygook Be Gone: Now Is the Time for Plain Talk,   http://communico.com/Resources/Articles/Customer-Service-Communication-Coaching-Skills/Gobbledygook-Be-Gone.aspx

21. Hubspot blog, Funny Tweets & Social Media Examples from 17 Real Brands, https://blog.hubspot.com/marketing/funny-brands-social-media

22. Hubspot blog, Funny Tweets & Social Media Examples from 17 Real Brands, https://blog.hubspot.com/marketing/funny-brands-social-media

23. BrainyQuote, www.brainyquote.com/quotes/victor_borge_100429

CHAPTER

7

Move Beyond Storytelling to Storydoing

Tell me a fact and I'll learn. Tell me the truth and I'll believe.
But tell me a story and it will live in my heart forever.

Indian Proverb

Your Brain on a Story

We all love a good story . . . and neuroscience has proven why. Storytelling has a powerful effect on our brains, triggering an array of biological responses and emotions that help us connect to, be moved by, and remember the story.

When great stories are told, two primary neurochemicals go to work. Cortisol is released when something captures our attention, like distress or conflict, keeping us involved and engaged in the narrative. Oxytocin, dubbed the wonder drug of storytelling, kicks in as the audience identifies with the main character/s, evoking empathy and a narrative transportation that creates engagement and can move people to a desired action. Experts confirm that engaging stories result in a better understanding—and better recall—of key points.

In addition, a good story fires mirror neurons, which light up specific parts of our brain that "mirror" what's happening in the story. So if the story is describing a specific smell, our olfactory system reacts, movement in the story triggers our motor cortex, even emotions conveyed in a story evoke those same feelings. This enables the listener to truly experience what's happening in the story.

For all of these reasons, storytelling can be the pathway to making connections and igniting engagement—key elements of authentic marketing.

When a story is shared, the audience feels the story, our whole brain is activated, and meaning is extracted. The meaning of the story comes from the personal connections the audience feels when they're listening to the story. When a story is well told, they are able to feel connected not just to the story, but the storyteller.[1]

Jennifer Aaker, Marketing Professor,
Stanford University

But what does it take to be a good storyteller, the kind who elicits those powerful neurological responses? Unfortunately, storytelling has become an overused buzzword that has lost its true meaning. The secret is to move beyond empty storytelling to a more genuine form.

Move to Storydoing

While this term may sound like marketing speak, what it's really about is moving your organization from telling stories to actually being an active part of them. This is all about showing what your company is *doing* to impact a problem, to make the world a better place . . . and it's powerful stuff.

When you are genuinely doing good for the world, you have all of the components of a great story:

- A serious problem that needs to be fixed
- People, animals, or a part of the world/environment that's harmed by those problems
- Creative interventions, technologies, or solutions that address those issues
- Heroes who give of themselves to help others
- Outcomes that positively impact mankind or the planet in some way

Your job is to take those components and creatively bring that story to life in a genuine, compelling, and emotive way. This is at the very heart of authentic marketing. You must *let go of some of your marketing instincts*. If your approach to telling stories always ends with a punch line about your company's product or service, you need to abandon that and embrace a more pure, more authentic way. You should also eliminate those old tactics of interruption and manipulation.

I spoke with Alex Jutkowitz, CEO, Hill + Knowlton U.S. and author of *The Strategic Storyteller: Content Marketing in the Age of the Educated Consumer*, to get his insights on storytelling. Here's what he said:

> One of the focus points for companies is to move away from a disruption model to one of seamlessness. This is where storytelling is a seamless part of everything that's done and happens all the time. It's less about communicating or marketing disruption. Disruption is passé. It's very difficult, expensive to pull off, and it's an over-used concept. We need to be seamless and just introduce things as a natural part of the lives of the audiences we're trying to reach.

Seamless storytelling takes shape in a variety of ways and places. For example, it involves how your story is portrayed in a brick and mortar store if your company is in retail. It also includes telling your moral purpose story on your website through engaging stories people want to read. Reaching people in the digital landscape with content they're drawn to and interested in sharing, such as a quick video about the impact of your moral purpose on an individual or community, is another way to do this. And don't forget about having genuine conversations on social media about your story.

Once you know the storyline of your moral purpose, you need to build a thematic narrative that serves as an umbrella for all of the stories you tell. This approach will bring consistent context to your stories and tie them together with a common and compelling thread. Your narrative will transform your story into knowledge for your audiences and should include key elements, which can be tied back to the new strategy model outlined in Chapter 3. For example, if you use innovative technologies to help solve a world problem, you should highlight those in the narrative. If your engagement approach is creative and gains traction, you'll have a strong story there as well. Both of those storylines would appeal not only to general news media, but to verticals as well, which expands the life and reach of your story.

Build Ongoing Stories

One-off stories that aren't connected to your narrative or grounded in your purpose don't anchor your brand to your focused mission in the world. As Jutkowitz explains, we must become ongoing storytellers:

> We all bemoan the ephemeral age of marketing communications. But what's the anecdote to the ephemeral? That's the ongoing story. That's a story that builds on itself, not traditional advertising, which was to look at the same 30-second spot over and over and over again until it finally sunk in. Nobody is going to sit for that anymore. We're all going to be able to block it or change the channel. So what do we do? We have to tell ongoing stories that build and have enough equity that we're credible. If you're an ongoing storyteller and you're a theorized storyteller, you have credibility. If you're a one-off or only talk during difficult times, or only talk during good times, you're a disingenuous storyteller.

Effective Techniques

Below are techniques for creating compelling, seamless, ongoing stories that bring your moral purpose to life and forge genuine connections with your audiences:

- **Tell It Visually.** Without a doubt, visual is the preferred format today. Think about how often we tap on our phones to watch a quick video, whether we're reading the news or buying a pair of shoes. With so many wearable technologies, people are perpetually connected, providing more opportunities than ever to communicate stories with visual mediums. Short videos, Instagram's newly released long-form video, a powerful photo, and VR are among the many options for visual communications. Facebook Live offers a way to tell not just produced stories, but stories in real time. Infographics are another great visual medium to tell the story of your moral purpose and its impact. Repurpose stories across multiple visual media for maximum impact.

- **Be Selective with Words.** Although visual communication is the fastest and most powerful way to tell your story, you will also need to communicate it with words. Select words that are vibrant, descriptive, evoke emotions, ignite the senses, and that draw the readers in, enabling them to feel and experience what's happening in your story. Stories well told will trigger those biological responses in the brain and make it memorable and meaningful. I also recommend that companies create a glossary of words, such as those that describe your company, its culture, its moral purpose, and its technology, to establish consistency when communicating stories.

- **Ensure It's Always On.** The story of your company's societal purpose will have a beginning and many chapters, but should not have an end. It should be a living, breathing narrative that evolves with your efforts. Engage your audience in your storyline by providing ongoing updates, even if they are as brief as a tweet. Show the progress you are making against solving a particular problem. As you bring the problem to life, your audience will crave more details about the characters and the heroes. Make your story one people want to follow.

- **Highlight Humanity.** This aspect to your story is the most relatable and emotional, and forges the strongest connections with your audience. Bring forth the people in your story, the victims and the heroes. Share their voices. Highlight the solutions and efforts underway and their impact on people, wildlife, or the planet. Do this in a way that reveals the concern and passion within your company to illustrate the humanity living within your organization, and also within the many others who are working together to address an issue.

- **Let Creativity Shine.** Creativity is in a renaissance right now. Just about everyone who owns a cell phone has at his or her fingertips the tools to be an artist, a photographer, a videographer, and a storyteller. Make the best use of those tools to tell your stories creatively and with impact across every channel.

- **Keep It Real.** Tell your story in an honest and genuine way and always with a little dose of humility and never any hubris. That's how people will connect with you and engage with your story. People will sniff out even the slightest hint of manipulation or marketing speak in these efforts. Resist the temptation.

Below are some excellent examples of companies getting this right. You'll notice they use many of the elements outlined in this chapter to connect with their audiences.

Warby Parker[2]

Eyeglass maker Warby Parker is a great example of using a beautiful and powerful visual plus a few compelling facts to highlight the tremendous impact of its Buy a Pair, Give a Pair effort. The engaging photo draws the viewer immediately and with very few words, highlighting how "The Power of One Pair" can positively impact a person's life. The copy then continues to show how helping one person can create a cycle of positive changes in things like productivity and income. This entire story is richly conveyed with one standout photo, a few simple images and minimal copy—very powerful and highly effective (see Figure 7.1).

The power of one pair

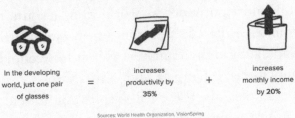

| In the developing world, just one pair of glasses | = | increases productivity by 35% | + | increases monthly income by 20% |

Sources: World Health Organization, VisionSpring

FIGURE 7.1 Warby Parker's website copy
Source www.warbyparker.com/buy-a-pair-give-a-pair

Gandys: Turning Tragedy into a Force for Good[3]

A "fashion for good" company, Gandys tells a heartbreaking and inspirational story on its website of two brothers who had a unique upbringing in which the family sold everything to travel around the world to explore and do volunteer work. When that journey took them to Sri Lanka, their parents were tragically lost in the 2004 tsunami. In honor of their adventurous parents, they formed Gandys, "a brand on a mission, a mission to stop people passively letting life go by when they could be doing more." The company supports its Orphans for Orphans" foundation by donating 10% of profits to help underprivileged children who were affected by the tsunami.

This story pulls the reader into the plight of these two brothers and their determination to turn a personal tragedy into something positive that helps others.

IKEA, Let's Play for Change[4]

This endearing photo (Figure 7.2) connects the audience to the joy that IKEA's play program brings to kids. You immediately get the sense that this organization values children and letting kids be kids. Part of the IKEA Foundation, this Let's Play for Change campaign recognizes that play is fundamental to a child's well-being as it builds new skills, promotes social behavior, and helps kids better cope with stress. The effort helps hundreds of thousands of children around the world who lack safe spaces to play, thanks to the work of six partner organizations in Asia and Africa: UNICEF, Save the Children, Room to Read, Handicap International, Special Olympics, and War Child.

I hope examples like these will inspire you to find creative ways to jumpstart your storydoing. Remember to use powerful visuals whenever possible, as they convey more to your audience

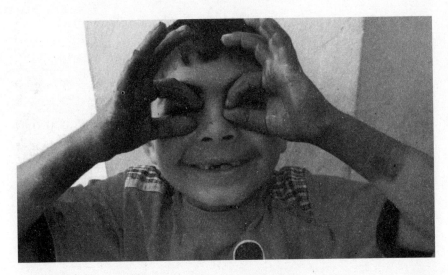

FIGURE 7.2   IKEA's Let's Play for Change
Source: www.ikeafoundation.org

than volumes of copy. Bring forth the person, people, or aspect of the planet your efforts are helping. Build a narrative and keep your story alive by giving ongoing updates. Most importantly, put your selling instincts aside and find your creative voice to tell genuinely interesting stories that highlight humanity. When you get this right, you're sure to trigger all of those powerful neuro-chemical responses in your audience, helping them to connect with, be moved by, and remember your story.

Notes

1. Persuasion and the Power of Story, Jennifer Aaker, Stanford University www.youtube.com/watch?v=AL-PAzrpqUQ
2. Warby Parker, www.warbyparker.com/buy-a-pair-give-a-pair
3. Gandys, www.gandyslondon.com/thegandysjourney
4. IKEA, www.ikeafoundation.org

8

Use Data-Telling to Anchor Objectives and Validate Progress

M oral missions typically involve lofty goals set against very complex problems. Therefore, it's important to outline reasonable, measurable objectives your company can make progress against. For example, if your goal is to deliver sustainability, you should outline what you can realistically accomplish in a certain time period and then track and measure it as you make progress. You may set yearly goals or longer-range goals. Companies do this in a variety of ways, depending on the types of initiatives they are undertaking.

This speaks to the importance of showcasing quantifiable data so that your company can validate progress made against your mission. This is the data-telling piece of your story. Data can be woven into the narrative to quantify the extent of the problem and impact of the solution. It can be used to create a simple powerful visual, chart, or graph, showing the progression of the impact of your solution over time, for example. Many websites illustrate their impact in a simple format with just a few words, and it is very powerful. Whatever form it takes, data will anchor your story with facts that substantiate the extent of good you are doing to combat an issue.

Following are several examples of this:

Walmart Sustainability Index

The retail giant is an excellent example of setting goals and tracking quantifiable progress. In addition to its sustainability efforts in its retail operations, Walmart also works to address potential environmental and social issues in its supply chain. The company's Sustainability Index Program "provides a snapshot of the social and environmental practices and outcomes in a broad array of products and supply chains." It was developed in collaboration with suppliers, leading NGOs, and the scientists at The Sustainability Consortium.

The Index gathers and analyzes information across a product's life cycle—from sourcing to end of use. Hot spots are then identified across the product lifecycle, along with improvement opportunities. Suppliers then respond to surveys covering issues deemed important. Data from the surveys are used to identify key social and environmental hot spots and to set an agenda with suppliers to drive continuous improvement.[1]

This type of data (shown in Figures 8.1 and 8.2) not only enables Walmart to better deliver on its sustainability goals, but also provides powerful, validated proof of exactly where the company is on that journey. For example, Figure 8.1 highlights

FIGURE 8.1   Walmart's visual clearly conveys the company has reached its sustainability goal
Source https://corporate.walmart.com/2017grr/sustainability/value-chain

that in 2017 the company reached its goal and bought 70% of U.S. goods from suppliers that participate in The Sustainability Index. It's not only impressive that the company reached its goal, but moreover that the company communicates this via a simple, quantitative visual that's easy to digest and leaves the viewer feeling good about the company.

Similarly, Figure 8.2 shows the Index Participation values, which demonstrate it is a robust and effective ongoing effort. Again, these quantitative outcomes illustrated in a simple visual format give the reader a strong takeaway that Walmart is successful in the sustainability of its supply chain. This is the type of story that all audiences—from customers to investors—have a strong interest in. Walmart's expansion from making its own retail stores sustainable to moving that effort through its supply chain demonstrates the strength of its commitment to this mission.

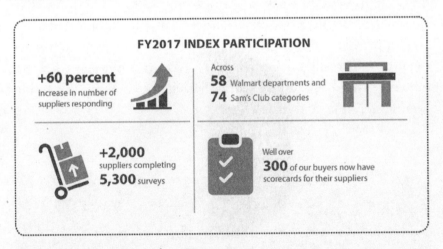

FIGURE 8.2   Walmart's visual about the number of suppliers who participate in the Sustainability Index
Source https://corporate.walmart.com/2017grr/sustainability/value-chain

TOMS

TOMS[2] is well known for its One for One® mission: For every product purchased, the company will help a person in need. The company's website features an ongoing calculation tallying the number of shoes it has given to children in need, which counts 75 million as of the day I am writing this page. Figure 8.3 tallies the shoe count. This image drives home the high volume of shoes TOMS has given to children in need. It also provides viewers with the sense this an ongoing effort that will continue to grow. Again, this is another simple visual using data to validate the company's moral purpose.

The company's expanded efforts include working to help restore people's sight, which tallies helping 500,000 people (through glasses, surgery, and medical treatment). Each bag of TOMS Roasting Co. Coffee provides 140 liters of safe water, a week's supply, to a person in need. To date, TOMS has supplied more than 450,000 weeks worth of safe water. TOMS has also supported safe birth options to more than 175,000 mothers.

Impressive contributions . . . and packaged well with impact to show real results. It's obvious TOMS was founded with this type of giving back in its DNA. That's key to making this brand honest, genuine, and likable.

FIGURE 8.3   TOMS One for One® Shoe Count
Source TOMS

Dow Chemical

A big company working to make big things happen in sustainability, Dow's 2025 Sustainability Goals[3] involve facilitating a transition to a sustainable planet and society. This includes seven ambitious goals, which are highlighted on its website in a video and in copy. When the company launched these goals, it outlined them clearly in a press release. Among the quantifiable promises Dow made were to "positively impact the lives of one billion people and deliver $1 billion in cost savings or new cash flow for the company by valuing nature in business decisions."

Again, this example articulates measurable, trackable goals over a specific timeframe, which means the world can hold Dow accountable for the promises it makes.

Siemens

This company often makes the short list as one of the most sustainable companies on the planet.[4] A quick visit to its website and it's clear why. Siemens has set an aggressive goal to be the first major industrial company in the world to achieve a net zero carbon footprint by 2030:

> The company is working to get halfway to that goal just three years from now, in 2020. This is an extraordinarily ambitious task considering Siemens has more than 60 manufacturing sites in the U.S. alone. In order to cut our carbon emissions in half by 2020, Siemens plans to drive energy efficiency programs, leverage distributed energy systems, reduce fleet emissions, and purchase renewable energy. . . . Fighting climate change and sustaining the environment is the right thing to do. And Siemens has the right people to do it.

Again, the company articulates clear, quantitative goals and provides the timeframe in which it plans to reach them. It's clear the company is serious about fighting climate change and doing its part to have an impact.

Levi Strauss

Among the company's multi-faceted sustainability efforts[5] is a goal to minimize water use in the production of its products. The company's website clearly articulates its mission, goals, evolution of the effort, and progress to date.

Levi's designers "challenged themselves to create the same great styles our consumers love with far less water." The result was a series of innovative finishing techniques the company calls Water<Less™, which according to the website can save up to 96% of the water in the denim finishing process:

> Since launching the Water<Less™ processes in 2011, we have saved more than one billion liters of water in the manufacturing of LS&Co. products. We've also saved 30 million liters of fresh water through the industry's first Water Recycling and Reuse Standard, which we piloted with one of our vendors in China. We're sharing these techniques with other vendors in hopes to see similar water savings.

> Most recently, we've taken our commitment to reducing water use in the apparel industry a step further by making our water reduction standards and tools, including our Water<Less™ innovations, publicly available to others within and outside our industry, and encouraging other denim companies—large and small—to use them in their production.

By utilizing our Water<Less™ innovations, we believe the apparel industry can save at least 50 billion liters of water by 2020. Our goal is to increase the percentage of our own products made with Water<Less™ techniques to 80% by 2020.

Infusing data in your story shows your company has measurable goals and quantifiable outcomes, all of which will serve to validate that your purpose is real and gaining traction. This will help build trust in the consumer, as well as excitement and a sense of personal satisfaction in your employees about being part of a company that is helping to make a difference in the world.

Notes

1. Walmart, https://corporate.walmart.com/2017grr/sustainability/value-chain
2. TOMS, www.toms.com/improving-lives
3. Dow Chemical, www.dow.com/en-us/news/press-releases/dow-launches-2025-sustainability-goals-to-help-redefine-the-role-of-business-in-society
4. Siemens, www.siemens.com/us/en/home/company/sustainability/business-to-society/sustaining-the-environment.html
5. Levi Strauss, www.levistrauss.com/sustainability/planet

CHAPTER

9

Infuse Trusted Voices in Paid, Owned, and Earned Media

We are a society in search of truth. As noted in Chapter 6, there's a collapse of trust taking place in the United States, caused in part by a "staggering" lack of faith in government. Additionally, media—search engines and social media—is the least trusted institution globally, reports the 2018 Edelman Trust Barometer.[1]

Moreover, the rise of fake news leaves society without "a shared base of facts," creating uncertainty and interfering with productive societal discourse, the report notes. Globally, nearly seven in 10 survey respondents worry about fake news or false information being used as a weapon, and 59% say that it is getting harder to tell whether a piece of news was produced by a respected media organization.[2]

> There is a desperate search for the terra firma of stability and truth. The fourth wave of the trust tsunami, the rise of disinformation, is perhaps the most insidious because it undermines the very essence of rational discourse and decision making. Silence is now deeply dangerous—a tax on truth.[3]
>
> *Richard Edelman*

With all of this uncertainty, people are increasingly turning back to experts as sources of trusted, reliable information. Edelman's barometer showed technical experts, academic experts, journalists, and CEOs have emerged as the voices of authority that are regaining our trust and credibility.[4]

Put Earned Media First in the Paid, Owned, Earned Equation

All of this points to the renewed importance of earned media, specifically of credible and trusted journalists. I have long believed it was only a matter of time before the pendulum swung back in this direction, with earned media rising to take its rightful lead in the paid, owned, and earned equation. Today more than ever, society needs informed, unbiased experts they can rely on for information about important and complex world happenings and for clarity around the volumes of information we are trying to digest and understand every day.

Of course, we have the challenge of distinguishing real news from fake news and factual reporting from biased reporting. The Internet has leveled the playing field in so many ways for the better; however, it has also provided a highly accessible platform for anyone to broadcast any opinion and for the wide distribution of propaganda and other forms of disinformation.

As such, the path to delivering truths involves identifying those media sources that are credible and honest and are committed to delivering news in a factual and unbiased way. This is essential for both individuals and for our society as a whole.

Those trusted journalists should be the primary focus of your efforts. With the public's renewed faith in credible journalists, they're a tremendous source for putting validated, authentic information out to your audiences about your company in general, and your moral purpose efforts in particular.

Focus on Your Inner Circle of Influencers

I'm going to start by giving the same advice I've been offering to my clients for decades. There are really only a handful of journalists and analysts who truly matter to your business. I'm talking about maybe 10 to 20 truly influential people who have the largest reach and the most trusted voices shaping opinions about your industry. These influencers often become brands in and of themselves. For example, in the technology world, I'm talking about people like Walt Mossberg, Kara Swisher, David Pogue, Thomas Friedman, and Sarah Perez.

Make sure you know who they are, what they cover, how they write, what their hot buttons are, who they like to interview, how they look at the world, and how they look at your industry. Know how to best communicate with them and understand what *not* to do. Read all of their articles, reports, and blog posts. Follow them on social media. Make connections with them digitally and in person, when possible. It's important to know their publications, but even more critical to know them. In a way, it's an acceptable form of professional stalking. You need to make it your business to know their business. They will recognize the difference.

A report from Cision revealed that 51% of influencers and journalists said that displaying knowledge of past work, interests, and beats are what drove them to pursue a story.[5] This is nothing new, but a good reminder. I've always advised clients that it's more advantageous to write one really thoughtful pitch customized to an important journalist than to blast out 40 generic pitches that are likely to end up in the trash before they're even read.

Reach out with stories and angles about your moral purpose that fit with their bent and their beat. If they cover things from a business perspective, approach them with that angle. If they want the human interest story, go at it that way. Quantify your efforts whenever possible and have plenty of third-party resources they can speak with who will be the voices that validate your story and make it real. None of this is new because these aspects of traditional PR haven't really changed all that much. The media have changed, the forms of communications have changed, but the right way to approach reporters has remained the same for as long as I've been in this business. The problem is that so many people just don't get it right.

Of course, today there are technology tools and platforms that can help better pinpoint these influencers, track their content, identify the events they're attending, and engage with them. Take advantage of these tools so your efforts are optimized for success.

Trust and the CEO

As people are not finding the kind of leadership they need from the government, they are increasingly looking to CEOs as leaders and voices of authority who can step up to address important issues. According to the Trust Barometer, nearly two-thirds of respondents want CEOs to take the lead on policy change rather than waiting for government. "This show of faith comes with new expectations; building trust (69%) is now the number one job for CEOs, surpassing producing high-quality products and services (68%)"[6]

Increasingly, CEOs are stepping up to these challenges, demonstrating a new class of corporate and moral leadership. For example, when Rosanne Barr posted a hostile, racist tweet, Disney CEO Bob Iger did not hesitate to cancel her top ranked ABC TV sitcom.[7] Even though this was the first number one show for ABC in the past 18 years,[8] Iger made this decisive and bold move, demonstrating the company puts its corporate values over money and draws strong moral lines no one can cross. This answers Darren Walker's (president of the Ford Foundation) "call for moral courage in America."[9]

A great example of that type of courage came from the actions of Ken Frazier, CEO of Merck, a $40 billion leader in pharmaceuticals. After a man drove through a crowd of protesters responding to white nationalist rallies in Charlottesville, Virginia, Frazier disagreed with President Trump's statement that 'There is blame on both sides." According to an article in the *Boston Globe*, Frazier resigned from the president's American Manufacturing Council and said, "As CEO of Merck and as a matter of personal conscience, I feel a responsibility to take a stand against intolerance and extremism."[10]

The article notes how Harvard Business School professor Bill George described Ken Frazier as being driven by both business imperative and by moral leadership. During the Ebola crisis, Ron Klain (Obama's Ebola Czar) tweeted that Frazier "put aside the bottom line to speed vaccine work."[11]

Today we are seeing an increasing number of CEOs banding together in creative and innovative ways to address tough problems. Case in point is the partnership of Berkshire Hathaway CEO Warren Buffett, JPMorgan Chase CEO Jamie Dimon, and Amazon CEO Jeff Bezos, which formed to create a health venture designed to tackle rising health-care costs.

Find those appropriate platforms and moments in time for your CEO to take a stand on an issue and showcase the values your leader and your company stand for.

The Credibility of Earned Social Media

Earned social media content from customers and other audiences is another powerful form of validation. And while the Trust Barometer reports that credibility has been declining in this area since 2016, recommendations from "a person like you" remain among the top three in terms of credible sources of content.[12]

Content around moral purpose efforts are a tremendous way to break through in this realm. This is intuitive. Content that is genuine, transparent, and shows earnest efforts to change the world for the better triggers those instinctive, emotional responses in the brain, which make people connect to it and want to share it with their community—all the things described in Chapter 7 on storytelling.

With the massive volume of information disseminated daily on social media, this is the type of content that stands out. Here are a few stats from MicoFocus to highlight the staggering amount of content happening every day on the Internet:[13]

- 656 million tweets per day
- More than four million hours of content uploaded to YouTube every day, with users watching 5.97 billion hours of YouTube videos each day
- 67,305,600 Instagram posts uploaded each day
- 4.3 billion Facebook messages posted daily

In a recent study by Stackla, 86% of consumers say authenticity is important when deciding which brands they support. Consumers are three times more likely to say that content created by a consumer is authentic compared to content created by a brand (meaning a faceless "corporate" voice). Most importantly, the study showed that people disconnect with brands that are trying to fake authenticity. Thirty percent of millennials have unfollowed a brand on social media because they thought the content was inauthentic.[14]

This speaks to the importance of ensuring your approach is genuine in the social sphere. Here are a few tips:

- **Listen and respond.** Use social media to have real conversations with your audience. That's the most authentic type of interaction you can have with them. That means you have to listen to what customers are saying and respond in a timely manner. Don't use corporate speak here. Have a real conversation, person to person. This will build relationships and show the human side of your organization.

- **Have employees become brand advocates.** Employees are a trusted voice within companies and the ones who are often on the front line of moral purpose efforts. As such, they should be empowered to share their stories, photos, and other content related to these efforts.

- **Show moral purpose in action.** Use social channels to show snippets of your moral purpose story. A powerful visual, a quick tweet, posts that provide updates—all help to bring this story to life as it unfolds and keep it top of mind.

- **Demonstrate consistent values across all channels and in every situation.** Companies need to showcase their values, what they stand for, and what they won't put up with. This is true across every aspect of the organization, and it's an always-on effort. When appropriate, use social media channels to showcase those values. It gives audiences a peek inside who you are and can speak volumes to the values your company works hard to uphold.

- **Personalize your posts.** When engaging with customers on social media, make it personal to them. Mention them by name. Show them you are having a genuine conversation so they see and feel the authenticity in your dialogue with them.

- **Put visuals before words.** People not only prefer visuals over words, but there's proof that they are actually more effective. Visual content reaches the brain faster and relays a message in a more understandable way than text. The brain processes images 60,000 times faster than it does text, so convey your messages visually whenever possible.[15]

As we look to the future of social media, I believe Facebook will remain the major platform for individualized mass media. In China, Tencent will continue to grow in popularity and rival Facebook on some levels. Instagram will remain on its path of growing popularity, taking the lead spot in its niche. Paid social will continue to increase, along with the use of chatbots. LinkedIn will become an even more popular platform for the voice of companies, providing a solid venue for CEOs to discuss moral purpose. There will also be a micro-segmentation of social media, so it's important to know who's using what. And visual communications will remain the preferred format among consumers. Keep on top of changes in the digital world and adjust your outreach along the way for maximum impact.

Owned and Paid Media: The Supporting Cast

Owned and paid media remain important, but play supporting roles to earned media. These channels give you full control of your story. As such, they provide a powerful means to bring those stories to life with compelling visuals and the many voices that showcase the real impact of your purpose.

As we look at owned media, let's start with your website's critical role. Invest the time and creativity into making sure your site tells the story of your moral purpose in a rich, impactful, and meaningful way. Think of this part of your website as inviting your viewers into the very soul of your organization, where you highlight your company's purpose in the world. Put your storydoing talents to work and make this the most compelling and emotional aspect of your site.

As discussed in Chapter 8, quantify wherever possible, use numbers that showcase the magnitude of the problem you are working to address and highlight the impact you're having. Most companies articulate very specific goals and their progress against those goals. Keep the content fresh, updating it regularly to show that efforts are ongoing and to underscore the progress you are making.

Blogs are a strong medium for keeping people apprised of your ongoing efforts, as well as sharing stories about the great work underway. They provide an excellent way to showcase how your company is living its key values every day. As CEOs are increasingly viewed as trusted sources of authority, blogs in their voice are particularly important vehicles to convey vision. With society turning to company leadership to be a guiding light and the agents of change the world needs, CEO blogs offer a means for leaders to address timely topics.

When it comes to paid media, how do you decide when and where to invest? Alex Jutkowitz, CEO, Hill + Knowlton U.S., recommends the following approach: "The first step is to see if you can create a story that can get attention, stand on its own, and gain acceptance through earned media. Once it achieves that and gets a little bit of lift, that's when you put paid behind it."

When you have that type of story, look to place ads in the digital landscape (versus print), make sure you showcase brand over product, and find authentic ways to connect with audiences. Ads covering the impact of your moral purpose fit that bill and are exactly the kind of content that will resonate with millennials.

When deciding which social networks to advertise on, determine where your content fits best with the various channels. And know audience demographics on various social mediums. For example, according to a report by Pew Research, there are more women than men on Facebook, Pinterest, Instagram, and Snapchat. For ages 50 and up, Facebook and YouTube are the most popular channels. Instagram and Snapchat are the most popular for ages 18 to 24.[16]

Native advertising is increasingly becoming the go-to paid medium. An article on Native Advertising Institute's website predicts that native advertising will drive 74% of ad revenue by 2021 and that brands will shift to mobile ads. In 2017, mobile accounted for a full 59.9% of all Internet traffic.[17]

Since video is the preferred medium today, it's important to understand the subtle differences from channel to channel before investing in video ads. For example, the majority of people on Facebook watch videos without sound, so adding subtitles to those makes sense, but nearly everyone on YouTube turns the sound on, so adding subtitles on that channel is not as important.[18] Length of videos matter as well. According to HubSpot, the ideal length of an Instagram video is just 30 seconds, for Twitter it's 45 seconds, for Facebook it's 1 minute, and for YouTube it's 2 minutes.[19]

Real-time ads have also become popular, with many companies serving up this format during sporting events or concerts, for example. Google offers real-time ads to take advantage of "micro-moments" and drive live engagement.

Since these media are in a constant state of flux, with new ones emerging and existing ones taking the back seat, it's important to stay on top of changes in this realm to keep your strategy on top of or ahead of the curve. Know audiences' current preferences and keep apprised of new tools, techniques, and features to make the most of your efforts.

Underwriting is another way to showcase your commitment to a cause related to your moral mission. Perhaps there's a special series on climate change on PBS or a show related to world hunger on NPR. In short, invest your dollars where they will deliver the most impact, are relevant to your plight, and will reach the right viewers.

Content Across Paid, Owned, and Earned

When your content is truly authentic and powerful, it can be strong enough to make its way across paid, owned, and earned channels. That's like catching lightning in a bottle.

One example of this is Lockheed Martin's "The Field Trip to Mars," which was the single most awarded campaign at Cannes 2016. This involved equipping a school bus with incredible high tech to create a virtual reality experience that enabled elementary and middle school students to look out of the windows and view a Martian landscape, instead of the Washington, D.C., street the bus was actually traversing.[20] Figure 9.1 shows the VR-equipped bus that took students on a trip to Mars. Figure 9.2 highlights VR images that enabled students to feel like they were actually taking a tour of Mars.

The ultimate goal of the effort was to reach students with STEM skills to "inspire their sense of possibility and ignite their passion for the critical skills needed to get humans into deep space." Rather than just tell students they could be the first people on Mars, they wanted them to believe it.[21]

This campaign demonstrates that when efforts are strong and stories are well told, they catch fire across all channels. Not only did the campaign will multiple awards, but news stories ran in publications like *Adweek*, *Ad Age* and *Mobile Marketing*, and appeared on social media channels, as well as on websites of the multiple companies involved.

Here are content and images from Lockheed Martin's website[22]:

The first people who will visit Mars are sitting in a school today. In fact, the first astronauts will arrive before today's kindergarteners graduate college. To help inspire these

FIGURE 9.1   Lockheed Martin Field Trip to Mars Virtual
Reality Bus
Source Lockheed Martin

students, Lockheed Martin created a one-of-a-kind virtual reality experience.

The Mars Experience Bus is the first immersive VR vehicle ever built and it replicates the Martian landscape. Riders experience a virtual drive along the surface of the Red Planet.

WATERisLIFE #FirstWorldProblems

Designed to raise money to bring clean water to the people of Haiti, WATERisLIFE was a powerful 60-second video campaign that leveraged (and attempted to end) the Twitter discussion #FirstWorldProblems in which people post about things

Figure 9.2   Lockheed Martin Field Trip to Mars VR image
Source https://lockheedmartin.com/generationbeyond/
mars-experience

like "I hate it when my mint gum makes my ice water taste too cold." It featured Haiti residents reciting those tweets with a backdrop of the poverty in that country. The video featured, for example, someone from Haiti standing in front of a dilapidated house reciting that he hates it "When my house is so big, I need two wireless routers." Figure 9.3 is a still shot taken from the video with the caption, "I hate when my leather seats aren't heated."

The campaign was highly impactful and went viral, garnering over 6.7 million views.[23] Not only did it grace major airwaves, but coverage appeared in publications like CNN, *Adweek*, the *HuffingtonPost*, *Ad Age*, as well as on social channels. The best outcome of all was that it generated enough money to provide one million days of water to those in need.[24]

Investing in Trust

As rebuilding trust becomes a top priority, we must find and invest in new processes, tools, and technologies that help to restore it. An example of this comes from the reaction to the rise of fake news. This issue has spawned the creation of new technologies, new algorithms, new tools, and new processes and the formation of new businesses. For example, Google now includes authoritative fact-checks in its search results.[25]Facebook enables users to identify fake news stories, is expanding its fact-checking processes, employing software to identify fake news stories, and is working to shut down financial incentives for fake sources.[26] Additionally, Facebook's news feed will enable users to see which stories are from reliable sources and which are fake news.[27] A new venture called *NewsGuard* was formed by two prominent journalists to address fake news by hiring dozens of trained journalists as analysts to review news and information websites in time for mid-term elections in November 2018. The service

FIGURE 9.3   Image from WATERisLIFE video to raise money for Haiti
Source The Inspiration Room

will provide online users with reliability ratings and "nutrition label" write-ups for 7,500 news and information websites.[28]

Companies must also take extra steps to prove their products deliver on their promises. This involves going beyond transparency to validating product claims with scientific evidence through third parties. This will help to combat the rise of false product claims that have come from companies like Skechers, Airborne, Activia, and Red Bull, among others. This type of validation helps build a base of trust in your brand and underscores your values.

In the future, we will need more processes and technologies that serve to deliver truths and restore trust. Stay on top of developments in this realm to ensure your organization is doing everything possible to strengthen the trust your constituents have in your brand. This is part of the moral code companies must embrace today.

To sum it up, have a thoughtful and solid strategy around paid, owned, and earned media and understand the key role each plays in authentically communicating your moral purpose. Place earned media, particularly working with trusted journalists, at the top of your priorities. Know your influencers well. It will take time to build these relationships and come up with news and story ideas that resonate with them, but that effort will be worth every minute of the investment. A single article in a respected publication like the *New York Times* or *Forbes* can not only put your company's moral purpose on the radar of multiple audiences, but also validate the good your company is doing for the world. Likewise, earning social media posts and shares through your company's act of good can help to earn your brand "likes" and, most importantly, trust. A smart paid and owned strategy will help support these efforts, providing controlled opportunities to tell your story exactly how you want to. Keep on top of micro-segmentation changes in social media so you know exactly how to reach select audiences and where. As these pieces come together, the story of your moral purpose will be optimized across the entire landscape, enabling you to reach and engage audiences with content that resonates.

Notes

1. 2018 Edelman Trust Barometer Press Release, www.edelman.com/news -awards/2018-edelman-trust-barometer-reveals-record-breaking-drop -trust-in-the-us

2. 2018 Edelman Trust Barometer, page 8, http://cms.edelman.com/sites /default/files/2018–02/2018_Edelman_TrustBarometer_Executive _Summary_Jan.pdf

3. 2018 Edelman Trust Barometer, page 3, http://cms.edelman.com/sites/default /files/2018–02/2018_Edelman_TrustBarometer_Executive_Summary _Jan.pdf

4. 2018 Edelman Trust Barometer, page 10,http://cms.edelman.com /sites/default/files/2018–02/2018_Edelman_TrustBarometer_Executive _Summary_Jan.pdf

5. Cision State of Media Report, March 2017, www.cision.com/us /resources/research-reports/2017-sotm/

6. 2018 Edelman Trust Barometer Press Release, www.edelman.com/news -awards/2018-edelman-trust-barometer-reveals-record-breaking-drop -trust-in-the-us

7. Chief Executive, Disney CEO Bob Iger Shows Moral Leadership Rose-anne Fiasco, May 29, 2018,https://chiefexecutive.net/disney-ceo-bob -iger-shows-moral-leadership-roseanne-fiasco

8. *Vanity Fair,* Yes Roseanne is Now the No. 1 Show on TV, April 18, 2018,www.vanityfair.com/hollywood/2018/04/roseanne-ratings-num-ber-one-show-abc

9. *Boston Globe,* Business Leaders Can Reverse the 'Implosion of Trust,' March 15, 2018, www.bostonglobe.com/opinion/2018/03/14/business -leaders-can-reverse-implosion-trust/bYNa50Ad4mL2Hy11lF5TeP /story.html

10. *Boston Globe,* Business Leaders Can Reverse the 'Implosion of Trust,' March 15, 2018, www.bostonglobe.com/opinion/2018/03/14/business -leaders-can-reverse-implosion-trust/bYNa50Ad4mL2Hy11lF5TeP /story.html

11. *Boston Globe,* Business Leaders Can Reverse the 'Implosion of Trust,' March 15, 2018, www.bostonglobe.com/opinion/2018/03/14

/business-leaders-can-reverse-implosion-trust/bYNa50Ad4mL-2Hy11lF5TeP/story.html

12. 2018 Edelman Trust Barometer, page 11, http://cms.edelman.com/sites/default/files/2018–02/2018_Edelman_TrustBarometer_Executive_Summary_Jan.pdf

13. MicroFocus,https://blog.microfocus.com/how-much-data-is-created-on-the-internet-each-day

14. Stackla,https://stackla.com/resources/press-releases/stackla-survey-finds-authenticity-drives-brand-affinity-and-consumer-created-content-influences-purchases

15. B2C, Visual Marketing: A Picture's Worth 60,000 Words, January 16, 2015,www.business2community.com/digital-marketing/visual-marketing-pictures-worth-60000-words-01126256

16. Pew Research,www.pewinternet.org/2018/03/01/social-media-use-in-2018/pi_2018–03–01_social-media_a-01

17. Native Advertising Institute, 7 Mobile Advertising Trends to Watch for in 2018,https://nativeadvertisinginstitute.com/blog/7-mobile-native-advertising-trends-2018

18. Native Advertising Institute, 7 Mobile Advertising Trends to Watch for in 2018,https://nativeadvertisinginstitute.com/blog/7-mobile-native-advertising-trends-2018

19. Hubspot,https://blog.hubspot.com/marketing/how-long-should-videos-be-on-instagram-twitter-facebook-youtube

20. *Adweek*, Inside 'The Field Trip to Mars,' the Single Most Awarded Campaign at Cannes 2016, July 18, 2016,www.adweek.com/brand-marketing/inside-field-trip-mars-single-most-awarded-campaign-cannes-2016–172531

21. Framestore VR Studio,http://framestorevr.com/field-trip-to-mars

22. Lockheed Martin,https://lockheedmartin.com/generationbeyond/mars-experience

23. COMPLEX, The Internet's Most Successful Viral Charity Movements, www.complex.com/pop-culture/2015/10/the-internets-most-successful-viral-charity-movements/rachels-ninth-birthday

24. Digital Training Academy, How #FirstWorldProblems was Hijacked by WATERisLIFE, www.digitaltrainingacademy.com/casestudies/2015/03/social_media_marketing_how_firstworldproblems_was_hijacked_by_waterislife.php

25. *The Bulletin*,Technology Helped Fake News. Now Technology Needs to Stop It, Nov. 17, 2017,https://thebulletin.org/technology-helped-fake-news-now-technology-needs-stop-it11285

26. *Scientific American*, What Facebook Is Doing to Combat Fake News, Feb. 1, 2017, www.scientificamerican.com/article/pogue-what-facebook-is-doing-to-combat-fake-news

27. *Business Insider*, Facebook Launches New Feature to Combat Fake news After Six Months of Testing, April 3, 2018 www.businessinsider.com/facebook-fake-news-about-this-article-feature-2018–4

28. *NewsGuard*, https://newsguardtechnologies.com/announcing-newsguard

PART

Reinventing Good and the Energy of Your Company's Soul

10

Creating a Purpose-Driven Culture

Customers will never love a company until the employees love it first.[1]

Simon Sinek

Answer the Generational Mandate

Moral purpose is the rallying cry of today's workforce and of millennials in particular, who are now the largest generation in the workplace.[2] By 2025, this generation will comprise more than 75% of the workforce.[3] However, the Deloitte Millennial Study 2018 revealed that nearly half of millennials plan to leave their jobs within two years.[4] On top of that, reports indicate there are widespread talent and skill shortages, making attracting top talent with the right skills a top concern for business leaders.

To remain competitive, businesses must understand this is not your father's—or maybe even your own—workforce. Millennials are completely different from baby boomers, who were driven more by employment stability and high pay. Millennials have different priorities, seeking to work for companies with the right ethics and the right efforts to do good for the world. A reminder of some stats on this:

- 85% of U.S. employees said they would stay longer with an employer with a high level of social responsibility.[5]
- 64% won't take a job if a company doesn't have strong corporate social responsibility (CSR) values.[6]
- 83% would be more loyal to a company that helps them contribute to social and environmental issues.[7]

All of these facts make moral purpose the new generational mandate . . . and it's more important than money or having cool products. It's the raison d'être that will ignite passion in employees by putting meaning in their work and the opportunity to be part of something larger than themselves. Companies must infuse this sense of purpose into the souls of their organization and make employees the lifeblood of it. Millennials seek to not only work for companies with good ethics and a strong purpose, but also those that enable them to roll up their sleeves, get involved, and fulfill their own sense of personal purpose.

A great example of this comes from Salesforce. The company's CEO Marc Benioff, widely known as a purpose-focused leader, has employees do volunteer work on their very first day of work. As reported in *The New York Times*, "On their first day of work, we take everyone and we show them the kitchen and the bathroom and their office and their desk. Then we take them out and they do service in the afternoon. They'll go to a homeless shelter or they'll go to the hospital or go to a public school. This is a very core part of our culture."[8]

Below are key steps that will create the kind of purpose-fueled culture employees will love:

1. Ignite employee passion, right from the first step

If your company is about to embark on its moral purpose, involve employees from the get go to ensure they're engaged and personally connected to the mission. Find ways to get their input, whether it's through surveys, focus groups, or meetings. Talk to them, ask them whether they get it, have ideas to contribute, are on board with it, and whether it seems authentic and will make them proud. Involve them in getting it off the ground—whether it's research, outreach, content creation, or other legwork. Make this mission something that involves all employees, so that it unites everyone around a common cause. Enable your moral purpose to give them a sense of pride that they work for a great company doing great things.

2. Live your purpose, enabling employees to *feel* it

Once you've established your moral purpose, make sure it's the real thing and not lip service given to a campaign designed to superficially satisfy this new mandate. It should be so powerful that employees feel its presence as a driving force in the company.

Diana O'Brien, Deloitte global chief marketing officer, explained the powerful presence purpose has within the walls at Deloitte:

> The Deloitte purpose is to make an impact that matters in the world for clients, our people, and our communities, and I don't think you could find a person in Deloitte that couldn't articulate that. It's embedded in everything and completely known by everyone.

Show that company management—from the CEO down—champions the effort. Demonstrate how they are living the company's purpose daily in their jobs, and find ways for them to share their passion for it. This is all about walking the talk. Anything less will be disingenuous. As an article in *Harvard Business Review* explained it, "When a company announces its purpose and values but the words don't govern the behavior of senior leadership, they ring hollow. Everyone recognizes the hypocrisy, and employees become more cynical. The process does harm."[9]

In addition to showcasing management's passion and commitment, highlighting purpose in action is key to making it real. As such, show management's involvement in the effort, celebrate key milestones of purpose, and make those highly visible to all. For example, if your work is helping farmers in Rwanda optimize their crops to better feed their community, tell that story. Or if your company just hit an important milestone in its sustainability efforts, make sure to celebrate it. Better yet, have the employees involved tell their personal pieces of that story.

Let actions and decisions prove that moral purpose is a top priority and a driving force in the organization. For example, don't make your purpose the first thing to go if there's a shortage of staff or money. Your purpose should not only be something sacred that is protected and preserved through all phases of your company's lifecycle, but it should also be the filter everything must pass through when making important decisions.

3. Make purpose permeate your organization

If your purpose is truly the soul of your organization, it will reveal itself in every aspect of your organization and become central to employee communications. This means that all levels of management should have purpose-focused conversations with employees on a regular basis during company meetings, team meetings, one-on-ones, and yearly reviews. There should be built-in feedback mechanisms (like quick online surveys or focus groups) so management can gain employees' perspective on the effort. This is not to say that traditional business matters, such as profit, new products, customer experience, and service don't matter. They are obviously essential for success. It just means that purpose and profit messages must exist in tandem, and if you lead with purpose, it will provide a powerful context with which to discuss other business matters.

4. Find your ambassadors

A select group of employees will emerge within your organization who will become lead advocates for the effort. You'll recognize them by their passion and dedication. When you find those employees, give them opportunities to tell their stories to others and to help engage co-workers. Their enthusiasm and passion will be infectious and help to build a community of ambassadors that will deepen the commitment to your organization's purpose.

5. Empower employees to make it happen

Make purpose one of the primary responsibilities of everyone's job and ensure they are set up to succeed. Make sure employees understand how to infuse purpose into their jobs, giving them the knowledge, skills, and training necessary to deliver on it. Do whatever it takes to facilitate their success.

6. Create a chorus of purpose stories

To bring the company's moral purpose to life, employees should be empowered to tell their personal stories around it. Enable them to share their part in the journey on social media. This will evoke a sense of personal pride in the company's accomplishments and their role in making it happen. They should have opportunities to share it internally with fellow co-workers, as well as online on social media. This type of content customers love to like and share. It also creates a chorus of voices about your mission.

7. Make purpose front and center when recruiting

The story of your moral purpose should be a lead element during the recruiting process. Highlight purpose in your job postings and early in discussions to emphasize the good your company is doing for the world and the critical role employees play. As stated earlier, purpose is more important than money to millennials, so make this a critical aspect of recruiting and not tacked on as an afterthought.

Lead with Purpose

Tough decisions need to be made not just with smarts, but wisdom; not just with business understanding but judgment; not just by listening but by empathizing; not just by giving orders but by inspiring. They will have to realize that humanity is central to being an effective leader.[10]

John Hillen, leadership and strategy professor, School of Business, George Mason University

A variety of forces have converged to reshape the role of today's CEO. Society is looking to business leaders to help solve world issues that our government is failing to address. Whether it's climate change, gun control, or human rights, people now expect the private sector to step up, take a stand, and take action. They also expect CEOs to place a company's moral purpose as its top priority, ensuring it is working diligently to change the world for the better. Operating with a sense of humanity and with powerful values like transparency, honesty, and empathy are also expected. All of this is happening during a time when trust is imploding and CEOs have emerged as one of the key voices of authority people are turning to for truth and clarity.

These factors demand that CEOs must effectively play a leadership role, not just within their organization, but within their market segments and the world at large. This expanded responsibility has created a newly defined set of criteria that CEOs must embrace to create a purpose-focused, value-driven organization that has a positive impact on the world.

Put Purpose First

Since the corner office sets the tone, establishes the culture, and determines the priorities for the entire organization, it's critical that CEOs are the number one champion of the company's moral purpose. Successful CEOs of purpose-focused organizations understand this is the soul, the driving force of the organization, and treat it as such. They lead with purpose in everything they do, demonstrating this is the *"why"* . . . why the company exists. An article in *Harvard Business Review* summed it up well. "If your purpose is authentic, people know, because it drives every decision and you do things other companies would not….."[11]

Leaders must infuse messages about purpose in their communications to employees, customers, partners, influencers, and stakeholders. When they demonstrate an authentic commitment to purpose, it has the power to unleash passion throughout the entire organization, bringing a deeper meaning to work. It can also create long-term value by building a brand that attracts employees, customers, stakeholders, and partners.

Diana O'Brien sums up the important role the Deloitte Global CEO plays in Deloitte's purpose:

> It all starts with the Deloitte Global CEO as the champion of purpose. He leads the effort every day, working with our Deloitte Global board of directors and senior leadership team. Having that senior sponsorship is paramount to the success of our effort.

Operate as Chief Values Officer

Humanity is becoming central to being an effective and respected CEO. As discussed in Chapter 3, companies must abide by a new moral code today, and CEO behavior must reflect that. Society expects companies to uphold strong values and demonstrate just behavior. While this includes things like honesty, integrity and transparency, it also extends to ethical practices such as the appropriate use of customer data (for the good of customers and not for profit or manipulation) and ensuring products do more good than harm to people and the planet. In this way, the CEO is required to take on this new role as "chief values officer," ensuring the company operates every day with the right values that are in sync with today's moral code. This must be demonstrated to both external and internal audiences.

When Salesforce CEO Marc Benioff faced the reality that his company, which was named 10 years in a row to *Fortune's* "Best Companies to Work For," had a gender pay gap, he didn't believe it because he thought his culture was great and didn't allow that kind of "shenanigans" to happen.[12] Also, Salesforce had policies that men and women should have equal pay. However, an audit proved the gender pay gap existed. "[The pay gap was] just everywhere. It was through the whole company, every division, every department, every geography," Benioff said.[13]

Following the audit, Salesforce spent $3 million in salary adjustments to correct the pay gap, with 6% of the company's employees receiving a raise.[14]

This reckoning with pay gap says a lot about what Salesforce is made of and what its CEO is willing to do to ensure it is doing right by employees. Admitting and correcting mistakes and injustices are simply part of the moral code companies must abide by.

Showcase Purpose in Action

When it comes to moral purpose, actions speak the loudest and prove your purpose is real. This means that CEOs should get their hands dirty and be directly involved with efforts involving the company's moral purpose. As the lead decision maker, the CEO must also ensure the company puts its money where its mouth is. That means making purpose a priority, which may require putting purpose over profit in some instances.

As referenced in Chapter 2, CVS made a bold, $2 billion decision to put purpose over profit when it decided to stop selling cigarettes in 2014. Stating it was the right thing to do for customers and the company, CEO Larry Merlo added, "put simply, the sale of tobacco products is inconsistent with our purpose."[15]

In addition to taking action around moral purpose, companies also speak out on issues impacting America and the world. For example, many CEOs spoke out to condemn the Trump Administration for splitting up migrant families (prior to Trump reversing this course) in the summer of 2018.

As reported in the *New York Times*: "'I think that what's happening is inhumane, it needs to stop,' said Timothy D. Cook, Apple's chief executive. Uber's chief, Dara Khosrowshahi, called the policy 'just plain wrong.' The Business Roundtable, a group of chief executives that Lloyd C. Blankfein once co-chaired, described the separation of children from their parents as 'cruel and contrary to American values.'"[16]

Infuse Purpose into the Entire C Suite, as Well as Middle Management

Although the CEO is, without a doubt, the chief commander of purpose, it must be embraced by the entire C suite and middle management for it to be a true driving force in an organization. In this way, every manager must be a leader of purpose, specifically to his or her staff. That means they must show their own passion and commitment to contributing to the company's purpose, while empowering their staff to do the same. This is how purpose becomes a powerful thread woven throughout the culture and the entire organization.

Partner for Purpose

One of the hallmarks of effective leaders is the knowledge and acceptance that they can't do everything alone. Strong leaders recognize that by fusing a variety of skill sets, outcomes are often more successful and more efficient. This holds true when it comes to purpose. So, for example, once a company determines its purpose, it may have part of the problem solved, but need another organization (or several organizations) to fully deliver on the mission. In this way, purpose can cut across multiple verticals, bringing together companies from disparate industries that otherwise might never have had the opportunity to collaborate. For example, if your company develops a vaccine that helps protect people from diseases like measles, TB, diphtheria, polio, etc., and you want to donate those critical vaccines to children in third-world countries, partnering with organizations like the Red Cross, UNICEF, or the World Health Organization can help expedite the distribution and implementation process. The Bill and Melinda Gates Foundation, for example, lists several partners—from the World Health Organization to UNICEF—on its site that help deliver on its goal, which is "to prevent more than 11 million deaths, 3.9 million disabilities, and 264 million illnesses by 2020 through high, equitable, and sustainable vaccine coverage and support for polio eradication."[17]

TOMS' website has an entire section called "Thoughtful Partnerships," which recognizes the Giving Partners that help fulfill the company's One for One® promise. The company then lists the qualities it looks for in partner companies, such as sustainability, locally staffed companies with a commitment to regions where they work, and companies that can provide valuable feedback that helps TOMS evolve and improve.[18]

For example, the company's "Shoe Giving" (One for One®) effort works because TOMS has long-term partner companies (Giving Partners) that place orders for the right sizes, quantities, and types of shoes needed by the recipients. TOMS sends the shoes to its Giving Partners, who place the shoes directly on children's feet.[19]

Walmart also partners with several organizations to strengthen the global supply chain. Here are some words from the company's website on its philosophy, which illustrate the importance of partnering to bring about positive change:

> While we leverage our size and scale to influence positive change in a variety of ways, risks and issues in consumer goods supply chains cannot be solved through the actions of any one company alone. Through our ongoing work with suppliers, industry stakeholders, and partner organizations, we're helping to strengthen the global supply chain at a much faster rate than would be possible on our own.[20]

Inspiring Words from CEOs

A number of CEOs around the world are stepping into this new role with clarity and conviction. Below are words of wisdom about operating with a higher purpose:[21]

> I think if the people who work for a business are proud of the business they work for, they'll work that much harder, and therefore, I think turning your business into a real force for good is good business sense as well.
>
> *Richard Branson, Virgin*

> When you're surrounded by people who share a passionate commitment around a common purpose, anything is possible.
>
> *Howard Schultz, Starbucks*

Money motivates neither the best people, nor the best in people. It can move the body and influence the mind, but it cannot touch the heart or move the spirit; that is reserved for belief, principle, and morality.

Dee Hock, Visa

People want to do well and do good. They want to understand how they're making a difference in the world. Things change all the time, but your organization's purpose transcends any individual product or service.

Mark Weinberger, EY

Make meaning not money.

Brian Scudamore, O2E Brands

An organization's culture of purpose answers the critical questions of who it is and why it exists. They have a culture of purpose beyond making a profit.

Punit Renjen, Deloitte

We're living in a time when it's so important for business to drive this new economy, this new view, this aspirational future of business as a force for good.[22]

Rose Marcario, CEO, Patagonia

At the end of the day leaders have to be authentic. And the only way to do that is to learn from other great leaders and make those lessons your own.[23]

Bill McDermott, CEO, SAP

The most important takeaways from this chapter are that purpose comes from the inside and starts at the very top of the organization. It's not a veneer or a superficial campaign to make the company look good. It's something that should run through every fiber of the organization and live within every employee, from the CEO down. When it's truly genuine, it will be a driving force in the organization that will produce positive outcomes for the world and for your brand.

Notes

1. Simon Sinek, https://twitter.com/simonsinek/status/4565458861436436 49?lang=en-generation-us-labor-force

2. Pew Research, www.pewresearch.org/fact-tank/2018/04/11/millennials -largest

3. *Talent Economy*, Millennials Want Workplaces with Social Purpose, How Does Your Company Measure Up?, February 20, 2018, www.talenteconomy .io/2018/02/20/millennials-want-workplaces-social-purpose-company -measure

4. Deloitte, The Deloitte Millennial Survey, https://www2.deloitte.com /global/en/pages/about-deloitte/articles/millennialsurvey.html

5. Sustainable Brands, Winning Over the Purpose-Focused Employee, February 8, 2018, www.sustainablebrands.com/news_and_views/marketing _comms/dr_john_izzo/winning_over_purpose-focused_employee

6. Cone Communications, www.conecomm.com/research-blog/2016-millennial -employee-engagement-study

7. Cone Communications, www.conecomm.com/research-blog/2016-millennial -employee-engagement-study

8. *The New York Times*, "Marc Benioff of Salesforce: 'Are We Not All Connected?'", June 15, 2018, www.nytimes.com/2018/06/15/business/marc -benioff-salesforce-corner-office.html

9. *Harvard Business Review*, When Work Has Meaning, July/August 2018, page 81

10. *MarketWatch*, Facebook's Mark Zuckerberg Could Use a Chief Philosophy Officer, May 3, 2018, www.marketwatch.com/story/facebooks-mark -zuckerberg-could-use-a-chief-philosophy-officer-2018–05–03

11. *Harvard Business Review*, When Work Has Meaning, July/August 2018, page 82

12. Salesforce website, www.salesforce.com/blog/2018/02/salesforce-fortune -100-best-companies-to-work.html

13. *Observer*, Salesforce CEO Marc Benioff Discusses the Unexplained Pay Gap in Tech, http://observer.com/2018/04/salesforce-ceo-marc-benioff -unexplained-gender-pay-gap

14. *Observer,* Salesforce CEO Marc Benioff Discusses the Unexplained Pay Gap in Tech, http://observer.com/2018/04/salesforce-ceo-marc-benioff-unexplained-gender-pay-gap

15. *Harvard Business Review,*Lessons From Companies that Purpose Ahead of Short-Term Profits, https://hbr.org/2016/06/lessons-from-companies-that-put-purpose-ahead-of-short-term-profits

16. *The New York Times,*AS CEOs Condemn Splitting up Migrant Families, Goldman Chief Defends Trump, June 20, 2018, www.nytimes.com/2018/06/19/business/immigration-borders-executives-reaction-trump-goldman-blankfein.html?emc=edit_nn_20180620&nl=morning-briefing&nlid=8541339020180620&te=1

17. Gates Foundation, www.gatesfoundation.org/What-We-Do/Global-Development/Vaccine-Delivery

18. TOMS, www.toms.com/thoughtful-partners

19. TOMS, www.toms.com/shoe-partners

20. Walmart, https://corporate.walmart.com/sourcing/collaboration

21. *Forbes,*The Top 15 CEO Quotes About Operating with a Higher Purpose, www.forbes.com/sites/danpontefract/2016/05/03/the-top-15-ceo-quotes-about-operating-with-a-higher-purpose/#244dd6523e72

22. *Fast Company,*How Patagonia Grows Every Time it Amplifies its Social Mission, February 21, 2018, www.fastcompany.com/40525452/how-patagonia-grows-every-time-it-amplifies-its-social-mission

23. *Inc.,* 7 Leadership Lessons from the CEO of a Multibillion-Dollar Company, www.inc.com/john-eades/7-leadership-lessons-from-the-ceo-of-a-multi-billion-dollar-company.html

11

Measuring the Legitimacy and Managing the Value of Purpose

If you can't measure it, you can't manage it.[1]

Peter Drucker

With purpose becoming the new currency of this era, it needs to be actively measured and managed, like all core business activities. In articulating its purpose, a company needs to be able to answer two core questions: Is the purpose believable? How should the purpose be managed to deliver business results? It is important to understand that currently 70% of the general public *will not* give even the most reputable companies the benefit of the doubt.[2] A company that states a purpose that is not believed to be legitimate will be left behind. It will not capture the long-term value that BlackRock CEO Laurence Fink spoke to in his letter to CEOs, which included a call to action on purpose:

> The time has come for a new model of shareholder engagement—one that strengthens and deepens communication between shareholders and the companies that they own. *I have written before* that companies have been too focused on quarterly results; similarly, shareholder engagement has been too focused on annual meetings and proxy votes. If engagement is to be meaningful and productive—if we collectively are going to focus on benefitting shareholders instead of wasting time and money in proxy fights—then engagement needs to be a year-round conversation about improving long-term value.[3]

This forward-thinking message is powerful, but we need metrics to understand how purpose is impacting long-term value. In stating its purpose, a company is creating a set of expectations and must know whether it is being perceived as fulfilling them.

In this chapter, we'll look at various methods for measuring the legitimacy and managing the value of purpose.

Measuring Corporate Purpose

An effective way to understand whether a company is delivering on its purpose is through evaluating the perception of its reputation. Reputation Institute, a global organization that manages and measures reputation, helps companies see into this powerful lens through its Global RepTrak® methodology, which assesses the emotional (how stakeholders feel), behavioral (what stakeholders do), and rational (what they think) responses to a company's reputation (see Figure 11.1).

The company's methodology provides insights into how a company's purpose is perceived across all stakeholders, including customers, employees, users, the financial community, channels, journalists, government/policy makers, opinion elites/thought leaders, etc., and offers a basis of comparison. This enables a

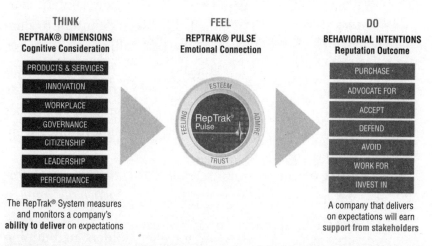

THINK	FEEL	DO
REPTRAK® DIMENSIONS **Cognitive Consideration**	**REPTRAK® PULSE** **Emotional Connection**	**BEHAVIORIAL INTENTIONS** **Reputation Outcome**

THINK: PRODUCTS & SERVICES, INNOVATION, WORKPLACE, GOVERNANCE, CITIZENSHIP, LEADERSHIP, PERFORMANCE

FEEL: ESTEEM, FEELING, RepTrak® Pulse, ADMIRE, TRUST

DO: PURCHASE, ADVOCATE FOR, ACCEPT, DEFEND, AVOID, WORK FOR, INVEST IN

The RepTrak® System measures and monitors a company's **ability to deliver** on expectations

A company that delivers on expectations will earn support from stakeholders

FIGURE 11.1   Basis for measuring reputation: RepTrak® Model
Source Reputation Institute

company to understand what is important to each stakeholder, how each stakeholder scores the company, and how the company compares to peers and best in class.

The methodology measures the perception of the company at three levels[4]:

- **The Emotional Connection.** *Companies typically establish a purpose to create an emotional connection to their brand, which is at the heart of what defines an organization's reputation.* Reputation Institute measures this connection through its RepTrak® pulse score, which illustrates the conviction and degree of support a company is garnering from stakeholders. Companies receive a score of 0 to 100, which is based on measuring stakeholder feelings of esteem, admiration, trust, and respect.
- **Behavioral Outcomes.** *A company's purpose should also drive stakeholders to be more willing to interact with and exhibit meaningful behavior related to the organization.* These important behavioral measures provide a basis for assessing an economic outcome, linking purpose to a company's potential to be more successful. These behaviors include intent to purchase, advocate for, defend in a debate, willingness to invest, work for a company, allowing businesses to not only align the outcomes of reputation to key performance indicators (KPIs) they may already be measuring, but also to project the economic impact of actions taken to more effectively manage reputation.
- **Cognitive Understanding.** *A company's purpose should provide the rationale for why a stakeholder emotionally connects with and is willing to act with a company.* Reputation Institute measures what is important for stakeholders in building a cognitive understanding and how they rationally think the company is delivering against those expectations. This

perception is based on their direct experiences with the business and what they have seen, read, and heard across all the media channels. The following seven dimensions provide a measure of how the company is viewed: products/services, innovation, workplace, governance, citizenship, leadership, and workplace. Reputation Institute helps companies understand how they perform in each of these dimensions of reputation and provides a comparison relative to the competition. These statistical insights can be used to drive critical business decisions.

As highlighted in Figure 11.2, Citizenship is among the seven dimensions measured by RepTrak®, which provides a clear picture into how aspects of corporate purpose such as societal influence, supporting causes, and protecting the environment impact the business.

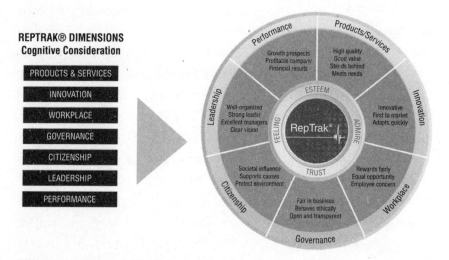

FIGURE 11.2 Identifying the attributes with the RepTrak Model that drive reputation
Source Reputation Institute

Since a company's purpose is a reflection of its DNA, it should be visible in every aspect of its business. A recent misstep by Unilever highlights this point. In May 2017, the company came out with new "body positive" packaging for its Dove Body Wash in the UK. The packaging came in different shapes representing different body types. The company faced significant backlash, as it was viewed as "patronizing women rather than celebrating them."[5] Beyond the packaging backlash is this larger issue: How does the company's investment in changing the shape of the bottle improve its sustainability? How did this product reflect the company's purpose?

"The Unilever example illustrates an important lesson," said Jay Manson, senior vice president, global accounts, at Reputation Institute. "The purpose of the company must be represented in all aspects of the business. The product and services need to represent the purpose. Innovation efforts need to advance the purpose. Employees in the workplace should be advocates for it. The ethics of the company should be defined by the purpose. The leadership of the company should represent the purpose, and finally the financial performance should demonstrate that the purpose is driving the company forward," he said.

Measuring the full 360-degree view of reputation provides a breadth of actionable knowledge that can be applied to important business decisions and strategies across the entire organization to understand how purpose is impacting reputation. For Unilever, the purpose of sustainable living is powerful, but until it is realized in all aspects of the business the company will not get the credit it deserves.

And here is the next challenge. Perceptions are in a constant state of flux, and stakeholder expectations of companies are changing more rapidly than ever. Therefore, a company needs to understand what attributes of its reputation are changing so that it can issue an appropriate response aligned with its purpose.

Other Key Findings from the 2018 Global RepTrak® Report

Through its 2018 RepTrak® report,[6] Reputation Institute surveyed 230,000 people in 140 companies in 15 countries and identified pressing issues and critical takeaways. At the top of list is that reputation scores fell in 2018, indicating the reputation bubble has burst. There is also a decline in both stakeholder support for companies and trust in companies to do the right thing. It is also more difficult for companies to attract talent, especially millennials, and harder to create loyalty due to a "crisis of trust."

Those issues create a pressing demand for companies to take the right actions now. That's where the opportunities exist to win back trust and enhance reputation. While fewer respondents were more positive about corporate reputation, half were neutral and open to being convinced. That presents an opportunity to appeal to and win over the "fence-sitters," while also working to win back naysayers.

The study cites that ethics, fairness, and societal influence (topics covered in this book) are the most influential triggers to enhance reputation. Taking the right actions, such as demonstrating equal rights, creating a positive workplace culture, and linking the enterprise to purpose are all critical here.

"A business has to be more than the sum of its products and services. Product quality, behavioral ethics, acts of fairness, and positive societal influence help build reputation reassurance," notes Reputation Institute's report.

Authentic communications is also critical, with CEOs operating as leaders who are "genuinely engaged with the world beyond your company's products and services."

These outcomes underscore the importance of the concepts outlined in this book, including having a purpose, creating a purpose-driven culture, operating every day with the right ethics and values, and having a CEO who passionately acts on all of those critical components. Companies embracing these dimensions must also actively monitor and measure their effectiveness, legitimacy, and impact to ensure they deliver the desired impact on reputation.

Additional Paths to Tracking, Monitoring, and Measuring Purpose

Beyond Reputation Institute's comprehensive approach to measuring reputation, there are a variety of tools and processes companies can and should employ to take the pulse of the impact of their purpose on an ongoing basis. Some of these are newer tools, and others have been around for decades, but they all can help monitor stakeholder responses to your efforts.

Customer Insights

Social Listening Make sure you have an ear to the ground on social media so you understand what you customers care about, talk about, and think about your business, your purpose, and your products. You can glean meaningful, actionable insights from conversations through engagement metrics and trend analyses. This effort will provide real-time data on how topics are trending. It will help you understand what's being shared most and get a view into the constant flow of audience opinions.

Sentiment Analysis Tools Also known as emotion AI, these tools leverage natural language processing systems to qualitatively measure your customers' "mood" about various dimensions of your business, including your purpose. By understanding how your customers *feel* in their posts, you can better analyze their reactions to determine what's resonating and what's not and know what adjustments should be made to ensure your purpose and other core dimensions of your organization are having a positive impact.

Data Analytics Tools   Use these tools to track metrics such as number of followers and to determine engagement in social media by evaluating the number of retweets, likes, video views, and shares. Click-through rates on ads, pages, emails, etc. are another metric to track. All of this will help you assess the traction your efforts are gaining with stakeholders.

Online Customer Communities   Offered by companies such as C Space, this effort is like a next generation focus group that enables companies to test messages, programs, and products on a community of online consumers. Businesses can gain quantitative and qualitative insights to ensure that everything from their products to their purpose is in sync with what matters most to customers.

Surveys   Although surveys have been used for decades, they continue to be a sound vehicle to discover customer perceptions and behaviors related to their purchasing decisions. Use surveys to find out what role purpose plays when they buy a product. Learn how they feel about your purpose and your ability to deliver on it. Is it meaningful to them? Does it make them feel good about buying your products? Would they recommend your products to someone else because of purpose?

One-on-Ones   Never underestimate the old-school method of simply talking to your customers. Design a quick questionnaire that you can use to guide you through questions about their views of your company's purpose and how it relates to purchases, brand perception, and loyalty, making recommendations, giving reviews, etc. You'll gain important feedback, show customers you value their opinions, and ignite deeper engagement by making the connection.

Influencer Analysis

Once you have identified your top influencers (media and analysts), conduct a message and sentiment analysis of media coverage and analyst reports to determine how messages are resonating and to identify your supporters, fence-sitters, and naysayers. You can use those outcomes to determine individual strategies for each influencer with the goal of building your base of supporters. You must also have a solid grounding in the perspectives of other influencers, such as contacts in NGOs and academia.

Employee Audits

Tools like Survey Monkey can help you better understand the impact of your purpose on job satisfaction, retention, and motivation. Find out whether your company's purpose resonates with your employees and makes them feel proud. Ask them if they think it's authentic and if your company is delivering on it. Find out whether they think aspects of the effort need to change. If so, ask them for their suggestions. This not only provides critical feedback about how your purpose is impacting your workforce, but also engages them in the process and enables their voices to be heard. In this way, it helps make purpose a community effort within the organization. The Patagonia example provided in Chapter 5 illustrates how the company secured employee feedback on its core values.

Expanding the Measurement Matrix

As purpose continues to become more deeply embedded in society and in business, we need to develop additional ways to monitor, measure, manage, and recognize it. Below are some "thinking-out-loud" possibilities.

As mentioned in Chapter 5, with the magnitude of data being collected, we'll migrate to newer processes that will allow us to manage and understand streaming data in real time. This "always-on" approach will help companies stay apprised of factors that drive customer service, product development, purpose, and issues that a company may take action on. Stay on top of new tools and trends that will help them analyze data in real time.

A Purpose Quadrant (similar to Gartner's Magic Quadrant) could be used to reflect market research on how various companies are doing against their vision and execution of their purpose. It could provide a powerful, at-a-glance view into the various players—the leaders, the visionaries, the niché players, and the challengers—to better understand and evaluate performance in the purpose landscape.

An annual Purpose Index could be created to measure and assess how the business sector is doing overall to impact problems, including how individual market segments, companies, and various geographies are performing. This could provide a view, for example, into how companies in select market segments (technology vs. pharmaceutical) are contributing to society, the top areas of focus for societal purpose (climate change vs. health-related issues), as well as areas in need of support. It could highlight year-to-year trends and outcomes for evaluation and analysis. This would give a view into the private sector's contributions to impacting societal issues and help shape decisions on future efforts.

Awards that recognize a company's purpose and its impact on the world are cropping up in pockets, but there's room for expansion. For example, could an organization like JD Powers create a rating system and distribute awards related to societal purpose? Could *MIT Technology Review* create an annual list of top uses of technology to advance a societal purpose? Could the Stevie Awards add an HR category on best purpose-driven culture?

The subject of purpose has been covered extensively in the media, particularly since Blackrock issued his call to action in January 2018. *Fortune*, for example, publishes an annual list of corporate world changers. Countless others—*Harvard Business Review, Forbes, New York Times, Time* magazine, and *Huffington Post*, to name just a few—have been covering various aspects of purpose on an ongoing basis. Expanding this type of media coverage will help raise awareness of the important role purpose plays in business and society, bring attention to what companies are doing to impact change, and motivate companies on the sidelines to get on the field. Most importantly, it will underscore the critical role purpose plays in business and how it impacts stakeholder perceptions and behavior and, ultimately, contributes to a company's value.

The critical takeaway here is that purpose, like other key aspects of business, must be monitored and measured to understand how it impacts what stakeholders think and feel, as well as how they behave in relation to your brand. Using the right measurement tools and processes will give you critical insights into how your efforts are impacting business results.

Up front, as you develop your purpose, you should make sure it is in sync with what your stakeholders care about. As you embark on your purpose, you should be regularly tracking reactions from both qualitative and quantitative perspectives. Annually, you should measure its impact on your reputation and the value of your organization. Stay on top of new measurement techniques as they emerge. These efforts will ensure your purpose is not only working to do good for the world, but helping your organization do well.

Notes

1. Measurement Myopia, The Drucker Institute, www.druckerinstitute .com/2013/07/measurement-myopia
2. Reputation Institute, www.reputationinstitute.com
3. Larry Fink's Letter to CEOs, www.blackrock.com/corporate/investor -relations/larry-fink-ceo-letter
4. Reputation Institute, www.reputationinstitute.com
5. *Today*, Dove's New 'Real Beauty' Bottles Spark Backlash, www.today.com /series/love-your-body/dove-s-new-real-beauty-bottles-spark-backlash -t111327
6. Reputation Institute, https://blog.reputationinstitute.com/2018/03/15 /what-it-takes-to-be-a-top-10-most-reputable-company-worldwide -in-2018

Make a Plan

I f you are ready to transform your organization around purpose, you need an actionable plan to get there. This chapter
provides a high-level blueprint outlining key components that
will help your organization identify, test, operationalize, communicate, and live its purpose.

1. Put the New Strategy Model into Play

Anchor your plan using the strategy model outlined in Chapter
3 to integrate your business, technology, and engagement strategies around your moral purpose.

Business Strategy

Start by articulating your business strategy. Most companies will
already have this in place. For those that don't, I'll top line it. The
business strategy highlights why your company exists (business mission), what it strives to become in the world (business objectives),
and how it's going to get there (strategies, tactics, and resources).
This process involves a number of analyses (SWOT, competitive,
customer segments, market dynamics, et al.), as well as developing a
plan for profitability and differentiation. Once you do this the next
step is to identify a moral purpose that aligns with it.

Identify Your Purpose

In most cases a company's moral purpose is a truly intuitive extension of its business—something in the DNA of your organization

that does good for the world. The steps outlined at the end of Chapter 1 guide you through this critical process. Make sure your purpose is aspirational and actionable. It should also be authentic and sustainable. Most importantly, it should make all of the stakeholders associated with your brand feel proud to be associated with it.

Invite a select group into this process who will bring the knowledge and perspectives necessary for a successful outcome. At a minimum, the CEO, CTO/CIO, and CMO should be involved, but consider others, such as people involved in current CSR efforts, key employees, a board member or outside consultants, such as those focused on marketing or business strategy.

Test It

Once you've identified your purpose, conduct research to validate you are on track. Make sure no one else in the market owns that exact concept. There can be similar ideas in the market, but not identical to yours. Since this represents the DNA of your organization, it should be unique to you.

If it makes it successfully through that filter, the next step is to test it on various audiences. This might include a select group of employees, a few key customers, board members, or possibly even an influencer in the marketplace with whom you have a strong relationship. This testing could be done through conversations, surveys, or focus groups.

Develop Your Technology Strategy

Once you know your purpose, identify innovative technologies that will enable your organization to better deliver on and amplify the effort. Next generation AI, analytics, voice recognition, supply chain software, apps, and many others may be among them. Some examples highlighted earlier in the book include Deere's use of software to help farmers maximize their crops to feed an ever-growing planet (Chapter 1) and China-based Ant Financial's Ant Forest tree-planting app, which is gamifying carbon footprint tracking for more than 450 million users in China to help tackle climate change (Chapter 3).

Craft Your Engagement Strategy

Determine a strategic plan to engage your audiences through your moral purpose. As outlined in Part II, to achieve authentic marketing, the approach should be genuine, transparent, and anchored in telling real and compelling stories around your company's efforts to make a difference in the world. It should be grounded in listening and focused on developing relationships through meaningful dialogues.

It should have a powerful always on narrative around your purpose that is brought to life via a variety of visual and written forms across all of the channels that reach your various stakeholders. Think about how the story of your purpose will unfold as you practice storydoing and tactics that deliver on it.

As you think through the elements of the plan, make sure you establish your key spokespeople (CEO and others), develop a base of purpose ambassadors inside your company (employees), and identify those top trusted influencers who will be your primary focus.

2. Establish Your Purpose Supply Chain

Once your strategic framework is in place, think through the various aspects of your purpose and the supply chain required to deliver on it. What *people*, *processes*, *products*, and *partners* will be required to be successful? Moral purposes can take a wide variety of shapes and forms, so this aspect of the plan will vary tremendously company by company. Here are the general areas to review as you work through operationalizing your purpose.

People

To infuse purpose inside the walls of your organization, you need to involve everyone and outline their roles. As discussed in Chapter 10, your CEO should spearhead the effort, but other members of the C-suite play an important part, such as your CIO/CTO, who will lead the technology piece, and your CMO, who will drive engagement. Employees are absolutely crucial to the effort, as they should be directly involved in bringing your purpose to life in their daily jobs. As such, you must determine their role in your purpose, and what training and tools they need to deliver on it.

Processes

Think through processes that have to be established to effectively deliver on your promise and to manage it. For example, you will likely need a system to track and measure the outcomes of your purpose. You may need to forecast and track expenses. Some efforts will require processes around distribution and delivery. For example, pharmaceutical companies that provide free vaccines to people in third-world countries would need to think through how products are delivered and administered. If you are going to donate a certain percentage of your profits to efforts that help save the environment, you need a process to deliver on that. If you have existing CSR/giving efforts in place, you should have a process to ensure they align with your moral purpose.

Determine the governance aspect of your purpose. How will you develop rules, practices, and policies that guide and control this effort? For example, should you set up a board committee around purpose? An example of that is IBM's Value and Policy board, which was formed to recommend policies and principles.

Products

Here you need to think about whether your purpose will impact products or services offered by your organization. Does your purpose require your organization to modify existing offerings, develop new ones, or ramp up production? For example, part of Warby Parker's Buy a Pair, Give a Pair effort involves giving school children glasses when teachers identify issues,[1] so they would need to factor in production of those glasses.

As outlined in your technology strategy, what innovations will you leverage to make your purpose more powerful, efficient, and effective? Develop a plan on the resources required to ensure these technologies are in place and effectively powering your purpose.

Partners

You may also need to align with a partner or multiple partners to deliver your purpose, particularly if there are holes in your supply chain that would be most efficiently filled by an outside organization. A good example here is TOMs. Through its One for One® program, the company gives shoes to children in need. It has more than 90 partner organizations, called "Giving Partners," which distribute shoes directly to children in need in more than 70 countries.[2]

Countless other companies, such as Walmart, Patagonia, and Seventh Generation, partner with organizations to execute on aspects of their purpose.

3. Launch Your Purpose

When your strategies and supply chain elements are in place, you are ready to go live with your purpose. This section provides a general framework for elements involved in launching your purpose and engaging your audiences with authentic marketing that will drive deeper engagement.

Constituency Mapping

Start by thinking through your various audiences and determining how you'll communicate the news of your purpose. Make sure *employees* know first, so they are informed and ready to answer questions that might come from customers or others.

While the next step varies, for this type of news, all other audiences can be informed on the same day. *Media/industry analysts* should be informed via a press release and customized email or via a DM on social channels, depending on how you communicate with each of them.

You should send an email to *customers* letting them know about this new endeavor. Since purpose has become a driver in purchasing decisions, your customer base should embrace this news.

You could also consider that same type of outreach to other "friends" of the company, such as *partner companies, industry associations, organizations, other thought leaders* in your industry, or those involved in your particular cause/purpose.

Start Your Authentic Content Engine

When you launch your effort, you are telling the first chapter of your story. That said, if there is a legacy value in your company that ties into your purpose, your story should reflect that, as it underscores how it is deeply embedded in your DNA. This content should articulate your "why." Showcase the issue your company is addressing, why it matters to your organization, and why you are working to solve it. Show the human side of your organization, its passion and commitment to your purpose, and reveal your raison d'être.

Set measurable goals right from the outset and commit to tracking progress against them. Chapter 8 on data-telling provides an overview of how companies are doing that.

Develop Communications Standards

You may want to consider developing a communications standards manual around your purpose, which will serve as a guide on language, key messages, use of visuals, etc. This will help to keep your content consistent and focused. As you empower employees to tell their own stories, it will provide a framework for that outreach.

Core Materials for Consideration:

- **Key Messages.** This document should include compelling top-line messages about your purpose that will serve as a reference to ensure content is consistent.
- **Website.** Your website should devote a section to your purpose, even if it's just a page. This is an ideal venue to bring your story to life with photos, key messages, and stories that will develop over time about your purpose. As you develop this website content, remember the rules about using visuals, descriptive words, and other key aspects of storytelling. You also want to be clear about the goals you have set and the timeframe in which you plan to achieve them.
- **Purpose Content From the CEO.** A blog post or video from the CEO not only provides a great vehicle to highlight the focus of your company's purpose, but also illustrates that

this commitment comes from the very top of the organization. A blog can also be a great vehicle for ongoing updates and genuine, compelling aspects of your story as it unfolds.

- **Media Relations Strategy.** Implement a targeted media relations strategy to reach and educate key contacts on your purpose. This would involve, for example, pitches tailored to their specific beats and interests, as well as a general press release that provides additional details (goals, partners, etc.) related to your company's purpose.
- **Social Media Content.** Start your purpose-focused social media efforts, creating posts for all of your channels to spread the word and engage with your online constituents. Empower your employees to do the same so they can share in the excitement of working to help solve a world problem.

Ready Your Spokespeople

The CEO should be the lead spokesperson for your organization's purpose. As such, make sure he or she is not only available for interviews around the launch, but also ready to speak passionately about it and answer questions the media might ask. If your organization has someone who leads sustainability or your moral purpose, that person should be available and ready to comment as well.

What's described above are the basics. You could expand this by producing a corporate purpose-focused video or creating an infographic that visually depicts the problem and your solution. Paid content such as native advertising is another element to consider.

As your story unfolds, you will have many other chapters to add that can be told in various formats, from a tweet to video. Engage the readers by bringing them into the problem you are addressing, the great work underway, and the impact you are having on the planet. Remember to use the principles outlined in Part II to keep your content genuine, demonstrate the positive values that drive your organization, and show the humanity within your brand.

4. Live the Purpose Promise

As your organization begins to live its promise, you must ensure it gains traction, remains relevant, stays authentic, and reaches the key goals you set at the outset.

Tracking, Measuring, and Reporting

To the point above, it is critical that you track, measure, and report your progress against the goals you set for your purpose. Most companies with a strong commitment to their purpose explicitly highlight what they set out to accomplish and show actual progress against that goal. This is detailed in Chapter 8. This not only validates that the effort is authentic, but it also highlights the impact your purpose is having on people or the planet.

Always On Storydoing

Your story should be engaging and the kind of content your audiences wants to follow as it develops. Therefore, you must keep the story alive by giving updates on all of your communications channels, whether it's a picture posted on Facebook, a video on YouTube, a quick tweet, a blog post, or an infographic that highlights your purpose and its impact. There will be many aspects of your story that will appeal to different audiences. For example, the technology innovations you use could be a story in its own right, along with your engagement strategies. Think through the many aspects of your story and work to share those with appropriate audiences.

Next Gen Issues/Response

Having a moral purpose can also extend to standing up and speaking out on world issues, particularly those that governments are failing to address. This is the new expectation of businesses today. It means that relevant topics should be followed closely to determine when it's time to go public and take a stand. We saw a number of organizations take a stance on gun control following the Parkland, Florida, school shooting, as well as around the issue of separating families immigrating to the United States. Determine what issues are relevant to your business and your purpose, follow them closely, and be prepared to speak out when it makes sense to do so.

Living Your Values

With humanity front and center today, it's critical that companies operate with strong ethics and values each and every day. As stated before, you can't do good in one area and behave poorly in another. Make sure everything you do—from how you treat customers (think about the incident when United Airlines dragged a passenger off of its plane) to how you treat employees and everyone else who comes in contact with your brand—is something you are proud of and that shows the human side of your brand.

Feedback Mechanisms

Deploy ongoing feedback mechanisms among employees and customers to ensure your effort is working, resonating, and authentic and is positively impacting perception of your brand.

Stick with It

Don't abandon your purpose in bad times or make it a flash-in-the pan effort. If it's truly part of your DNA, it should live within all phases of your organization's lifecycle. It can evolve and morph, but the core of it should always be a driving force in your organization.

5. Measure the Impact

As outlined in Chapter 11, measuring the impact purpose has on the value of your organization is critical. The outcomes from measurement will give you the insights necessary to understand whether you are on track or need to course correct. Most importantly, it can also give you a lens into how your purpose is impacting what your stakeholders think about your brand, their emotional responses to it, and their behavior related to it. Ultimately, this enables you to understand the long-term, sustainable value that purpose is bringing to your organization.

Having a solid game plan grounded in smart strategies will guide your organization as it evolves to become an authentic, purpose-driven brand. Use this plan as a general guideline, customize it to your specific organization and the purpose you've identified, and share it with the right people to secure feedback and bring everyone on board. Revisit it regularly to assess what's working and what needs to be adjusted to ensure your purpose is having the desired impact on your organization and the world.

Notes

1. Warby Parker, www.warbyparker.com/buy-a-pair-give-a-pair
2. TOMS, www.toms.com/shoe-partners

13

Purpose Is Everything

We are standing at one of those pivotal moments in time. A sea change is happening all around us that I believe will define not only how businesses operate moving forward, but more importantly, how we value them. Since I started writing this book, purpose has quickly evolved from a topic that was just emerging on the business world's radar to becoming the new mandate that is being embraced across industries and geographies.

Some companies like Patagonia, TOMS, Deloitte, Salesforce, and others mentioned in this book are way ahead of the curve. However, for many others, doing good remains a siloed, CSR initiative—a dated approach ready for this disruption. By embracing this transformational change, companies can unlock the power of purpose, find their humanity, and make this force of good a driver in their daily operations.

As described in Chapter 3, with the new strategy model of uniting business, engagement, and technology strategies around a powerful purpose, companies can deliver an entirely new level of value that will appeal to every audience, from employees to stakeholders.

Although discovering your company's soul is a journey, it is certainly a trip worth taking. As purpose takes root in our society, evidence continues to surface proving that companies are doing well by doing good. Study after study shows that purpose attracts and retains talent by giving meaning to work. This is the answer to millennials' "ask" and, as the largest generation in the U.S. workforce, it's an ask worth answering. This is particularly true today since finding the right talent is a top-of-mind issue for management.

Also, at a time when it is more difficult to create brand loyalty, purpose can be the catalyst that gives more meaning to purchases and provides that feel-good outcome to consumers. Studies reveal that consumers are even willing to pay more for a product if it is offered by a socially responsible company. As Reputation Institute reports, best practices among the most reputable companies include linking products to enterprise purpose. "A business has to be more than the sum of its products and services. Leveraging product quality, behavioral ethics, acts of fairness, and positive social influence helps build reputation reassurance."[1]

CEOs are also recognizing the value of marrying purpose with profit. A full 80% of Fortune 1000 CEOs believe that a company's future growth and success hinge on a values-driven mission that balances profit and purpose.[2]

An article by marketing intelligence service company WARC reported on a presentation given by Brian Deese, managing director/global head of sustainable investing at BlackRock, at the 2018 Techonomy NYC conference, which articulated how social purpose:

> [is] no longer simply a nice-to-have item on the agenda, but instead constitutes a fundamental element of future-proofing a business. For companies to succeed over the long term, they need to be able to define, and then defend, their social purpose in the communities that they operate in, with the customers that they engage with, with their own employees.[3]

I spoke with Jeffrey Bradach, managing partner and co-founder of The Bridgespan Group, which is a global nonprofit organization that collaborates with mission-driven organizations and philanthropists to achieve results in addressing society's most important challenges and opportunities. It was launched by Bain & Company in 2000.

Bradach spoke on the subject of purpose and investing, articulating a trend he is seeing in impact investing and the move for companies to prove they are delivering in both the realm of profit and purpose:

> Impact investing now has attracted a lot of attention with people doing a variety of interesting things in this realm. We're in an era where there are some people who are saying let's not just tell stories about the good we did, let's actually hold ourselves accountable about what it is we're trying to achieve on the impact front just like we would on the financial front. The business would be built so that it's delivering on both of those propositions as it goes forward. That's a growing field which is attracting a lot more money.

Like other eras that have come before it, a variety of forces have emerged and converged to evolve our world to this place. From governments failing to address important issues, to society using its loud and powerful voice to articulate what's expected from businesses, to a new generation that views helping the world as being more important than helping themselves—all of these dynamics have created this purpose-driven era.

With this change comes tremendous opportunity. Purpose should inspire companies to color outside the lines, forge new paths, and think more creatively about how to use their expertise to solve world problems. Organizations that embrace this have the potential to emerge as brands emblematic of this era . . . and those that don't risk becoming irrelevant. In the past, the things that defined a company have often been proprietary—an organization's "secret sauce." Purpose is the flip side of that coin. It should be open, shared, collaborative, welcoming. That's what makes it more effective, more powerful, and more meaningful. It's the humanity that exists in organizations, which emerges as they unite around a cause much larger than their own business. This is already starting to happen. A great example of this is the one I've referred to several times in the book, with Amazon, Berkshire Hathaway, and JPMorgan coming together to provide a much needed answer for better and more affordable health care for employees.

An inherent responsibility also comes with having a moral purpose and operating with a moral code. Delivering on and staying true to your purpose requires a deep commitment that starts at the very top of the organization and must live within every level of management and every single employee. If it is truly the soul of the organization, purpose will reveal itself in everyone and in everything a company does. It will not be turned on in good times and off in bad. It will be an ongoing force that unites people from all corners of the company—from finance and research to marketing and manufacturing—around a common meaningful mission. As such, purpose can become a source of innovation, sparking new thinking and ideas and possibly even the creation of new products and services. In this way, purpose can actually become a disruptor in its own right.

Operating with a strong moral code is part of today's rules of engagement. That means doing business ethically, treating people with respect and equality, and ensuring products do more good than harm. This involves operating with the right values every single minute of the day. Recycling, reducing carbon footprints, and embracing other green practices are also part of this code. Moving beyond transparency to validating claims by scientifically proving products deliver on their promise is also essential. In short, it means doing business with more humanity than ever before.

This leads me to the role of technology in purpose and in our larger world (one of four key strategies outlined in Chapter 3). When it comes to technology, I will confess that I'm a long-time fan and supporter of all things tech. However, I am also aware that technologies can have a downside—like invading privacy or replacing people with machines—but I believe if we are responsible about innovations and pledge to use them for the good of mankind and not simply for profit or manipulation, they will serve us well on many levels. Today's biggest tech innovations—AI, voice, advanced search technology, IoT, sensors, as examples—hold the potential to not only create tremendous business efficiencies, but more importantly, to make our lives easier and richer and revolutionize offerings in areas like health care. To that point, have you heard about the AI/robotics technology that actually enables people to use their brains to make their prosthetics move? And there's work underway on a prosthetic arm that can actually *feel*—truly amazing!

Today, innovations in technology are relentless and ubiquitous. The greatest technologies of our time are those that almost disappear because they are such a seamless part of our lives. When we use the voice text feature on our phones, we don't even think about it as technology. It's just something at our fingertips that makes our lives a little easier. It's astounding what today's innovations can do to enhance our customers' lives and to amplify moral purpose efforts. Therefore, every company in every industry should have a technology strategy that puts these innovations to work not only for business, but for purpose. This is one of the fundamental strategies every organization must embrace, whether your business is in aviation or agriculture.

The next strategy I want to discuss is engagement. After spending nearly four decades in marketing, you may wonder why I would write a book about purpose. The answer to this is what excites me the most and is at the very heart of the book. The discipline of marketing has been evolving over the years from tactics of pure interruption and manipulation to a more genuine, customer-centered approach. We've been learning to listen, to have a dialogue, and to create more meaningful customer experiences. Purpose is the catalyst that will push marketing to its most evolved, authentic, and effective form yet. When consumers believe in and are passionate about a company's purpose, the natural outcome is an affinity to the brand, which naturally drives commerce. When I think about my journey, which began four decades ago writing press releases about a new Rawlings baseball glove to today having the privilege of counseling companies like Deere on how to find its purpose to help feed an ever-growing planet, it's astonishing. This transformation is not only fulfilling, but elevates marketing to an entirely new level.

Stories about doing good for the world are by their very nature the kind of content people gravitate to, want to watch, read about, and follow, and ultimately like and share. And that's how your customers will help to build your brand, by sharing your content and hopefully telling their own stories about their part in your company's purpose.

Marketers must be mindful of putting their selling instincts aside, as stories involving purpose should be real, honest, and transparent. When you are doing good for the world, you are more than telling a story, you are storydoing, which is powerful stuff. It sells itself without any push. An effective purpose will give you all of the elements of a powerful story—problems that need to be fixed, people, animals, or the world being harmed by those problems, creative solutions that address those issues, heroes who give of themselves to help others, and positive outcomes that impact mankind or the planet. Use those elements—and your best creative talents—to bring your story to life and share them across the channels most relevant to your audiences. When done right, you'll ignite biological responses and emotions in your audience that will enable them to connect to, be moved by, and remember your story.

There should also be multiple layers of your story, which can be tied back to the strategy model outlined in this book. Start with a thematic narrative that serves as the umbrella and provides consistent context for all of the stories you tell. Then highlight the various elements that are the core components of your moral purpose strategy. How your moral purpose is connected to your business strategy is one aspect of your narrative; your use of innovative technologies to solve world problems and creative communications strategies that show how you engage your audiences in your purpose are other elements. This approach will make your story richer and highlight the depth and breadth of your efforts, while also giving it additional angles that will naturally appeal to various audience segments.

Making your brand more human is also critical to engaging with today's consumer. People today simply demand more of companies. They're tired of being talked at and sold to. They want to engage with companies that are more real, more genuine, and operate every day with values and traits they respect and relate to. Think about the qualities you admire in other people—and those your audience cares about most—and emulate those in your brand. I'm talking about things like being honest and transparent, having empathy for others, standing up for what you believe in, being provocative when it makes sense, saying you're sorry when you're wrong, and, of course, having a sense of humor.

Earned media is once again rising to the top of the paid, owned, and earned equation and, because of this, should be the primary focus of your efforts. We live in a world in which everyone is a member of the media in a sense, but you need to find those trusted voices that stand out in today's skeptical world. Credible media outlets can help you reach key audiences with validated stories about your efforts. When it comes to journalists, find the top 10 to 20 most influential and trusted media, know their beat, their hot buttons, and how they like to communicate, and then make it your job to get the right stories to them. Paid and owned will play a supporting role in your marketing efforts, so make sure you put the appropriate amount of time and money into the right opportunities.

Your CEO's voice is more important than ever, as company leadership has emerged as another trusted source of information. To that end, make sure your CEO is not only the lead champion of your company's purpose, but also the person who is most vocal and involved with it. There are also new expectations of CEOs, as society looks to business leaders to help solve world problems and become activists on pressing issues.

Jeffrey Bradach from The Bridgestone Group says:

> It's just been striking to me in the last 18 to 24 months that when you look at the #MeToo movement, the racial issues in Charlottesville, Virginia, or things related to racial justice and racial equality, that many businesses have been vocal aggressive movers when compared to other institutions in society, including government. There are business leaders in the vanguard of reaction to those issues, and that's also an important part of the proposition.

This point is supported in the results of Reputation Institute's 2018 Global RepTrak® study, which found that CEOs must be leaders who are genuinely engaged with the world beyond their own products and services.[4]

While purpose starts at the top of an organization, it must be woven through all of management. The CTO should tell the tech version of the story, and the CMO should tell the engagement piece. As purpose becomes more deeply engrained in business, new positions like "chief purpose officer" or "chief values officer" may emerge and will be central to this effort. The voice of your entire workforce also should be heard and shared, so empower your employees to tell their personal stories of delivering on your company's purpose.

That point leads me straight to culture. Don't embark on a purpose and leave your company's culture in its wake. Make purpose the thing that defines your organization—that makes it stand out in the world. Lead with it when you recruit and when you talk to employees. Make them not only hear it, but feel it. It's a powerful thing to rally around and can do wonders for your workforce's motivation and for everyone's soul. Make purpose the reason employees love your company and you'll see that reflected in what they give back to your organization ... and the world.

I believe as the roots of purpose become more deeply embedded in our society, an ecosystem of purpose will develop. All aspects of our culture will have a role in it, from businesses that will devote their core competencies to purpose, to people who will dedicate their time to it and support purpose-driven companies (with their voices and wallets), to the media who will continue to raise awareness of purpose to make it top of mind in our collective conscience, to the education system and business schools in particular, which will teach the next generation about the important role purpose plays in our society and in commerce.

I also believe purpose will become a catalyst for innovations that are grounded in humanity—whether it's new technologies, products and services, businesses or industries. As stated earlier, in this way, purpose can itself become a force of disruption.

If you're stuck on what your company's purpose should be, go back to Chapter 1 and review the questions. It may seem daunting to find, but I believe a company's purpose is most often right under its nose. Start by thinking about who or what in the world would benefit most from what your company offers. I find that prompt alone usually surfaces the best answer.

To spark some thinking, I'll throw out a few examples. Could Amazon use drones to deliver supplies during times of crisis or emergency situations? Perhaps a partnership with the Red Cross would make sense for this purpose. Companies like Facebook or Verizon could provide no-cost connectivity to bring access to everyone. How about a company like Oracle, the king of data, mining data to help humanity address a world problem such as hunger, poverty, climate change, or disease. Here, a collaboration with a social change organization like the World Bank would help maximize impact.

For a little inspiration on what purpose can do for your organization and every single person who works there, here's a quote from Diana O'Brien on the power of Deloitte's soul:

> When we built Deloitte University (DU), I had the amazing opportunity to run it day-to-day. What I came to realize was that it is more than a place to learn and for leaders to grow—it is the manifestation of everything we hope to be as leaders, which is to say we believe that at any moment any one of us has the opportunity to lead, to make a difference, to make an impact that matters, and great leaders don't do it alone. It is more than a place, it's a mindset, it's "something" that every professional carries with them. And when you go to DU, you get infused with the energy and passion of our professionals. You feel it happen because you're in a safe place where you are allowed to practice and make mistakes. You leave more confident in your ability to make that impact and more mindful that with it comes responsibility. If you went to DU, you would feel the heart and soul of Deloitte because it lives there.

As I wind down this chapter and book, I'll circle back to Aristotle's eudaimonia. This is all about doing well by living well. By unlocking the power of purpose, your organization will do well by creating value—long-term value—that's sustainable, which should be the goal of every CEO, every board member, and every shareholder. By living well, you'll provide work that's meaningful to your employees, give customers a powerful emotional connection to your brand, and help to ignite positive change in the world. Brought together, there's no doubt that today purpose is everything.

Notes

1. Reputation Institute, What it Takes to Be a Top 10 Most Reputable Company Worldwide in 2018, March 15, 2018
2. Covestro unveils new survey of U.S. Fortune 1000 CEOs on business and purpose, April 5, 2018,www.prnewswire.com/news-releases /covestro-unveils-new-survey-of-us-fortune-1000-ceos-on-business-and -purpose-300624494.html
3. WARC, July 9, 2018, Blackrock Champions Social Purpose, www.warc .com/newsandopinion/news/blackrock_champions_social_purpose /40719
4. Reputation Institute, www.reputationinstitute.com

About the Author

Larry Weber is a successful entrepreneur, thought leader, and author, who founded several leading marketing companies. He is the founder, chairman, and CEO of Racepoint Global, an integrated communications agency. He also founded Weber Shandwick, one of the world's leading global communications and marketing services firms; and co-founded the Massachusetts Innovation and Technology Exchange (MITX), the world's largest Internet marketing association. Over the past four decades, Larry has counseled a number of leading global companies, including ARM, AT&T, Boston Scientific, Coca-Cola, General Electric, General Motors, IBM, Deere, Kaiser Permanente, Microsoft, PTC, the Pittsburgh Steelers, SAP, and Verizon Wireless.

Larry is widely regarded for his forward-thinking insights on the seismic shifts technology has had on business and marketing. He has authored six books covering disruptive forces such as the Internet, digital technologies, and the new business imperative of social purpose, offering marketing strategies that drive deeper customer engagement.

His books include *The Provocateur: How a New Generation of Leaders Are Building Communities, Not Just Companies* (Random House/Crown Business, 2002), business bestseller; *Marketing to the Social Web: How Digital Customer Communities Build Your*

Business (Wiley, 2007, 2nd edition, 2009); *Sticks & Stones: How Digital Business Reputations Are Created Over Time . . . and Lost in a Click* (Wiley, 2009); *Everywhere: Comprehensive Digital Business Strategy for the Social Media Era* (Wiley, 2011); *The Digital Marketer* (Wiley, 2014); and *Authentic Marketing: How to Capture Hearts and Minds Through the Power of Purpose* (Wiley, 2019).

Index

Page references followed by *fig* indicate an illustrated figure.

Action Works program of, 12–13; Patagonia Survey Participant, 85–87, 189

Peer reviews, 71

Pepsi, 54

Perception of company: as always in a state of flux, 185; Global RepTrak's method for measuring, 182*fig*–184; Unilever approach to measuring, 185

Perez, Sarah, 145

Personal data. *See* Consumer data

Personality, 109–110*fig*

Pew Research Center, 90, 151

Philip Morris ad (1950s), 67*fig*–68

Pinterest, 90, 151

Pogue, David, 145

Polman, Paul, 9

PricewaterhouseCoopers' Academy Awards apology, 112

Private sector. *See* Companies

Production Era (1860–1920), 65–66*fig*

Products: efforts to rebuild trust in, 157; false claims about, 27–30, 93–94; Moral DNA exercise on playing forward, 17, 49; purpose supply chain component of, 199; take a stand to ensure positivity of your, 18–20; Unilever's Dove Body Wash, 185. *See also* Advertisements; Marketing

Profit: CVS anti-tobacco initiatives choosing purpose over, 31, 172–173; Deloitte findings on proof of purpose driving, 91–92; recognizing value of marrying purpose with, 210

Purpose blog post, 201–202

Purpose Index, 190

Purpose Quadrant, 190

Purpose. *See* Moral purpose

Purpose supply chain, 197–199

R

Racial justice and equality, 216

Real-time ads, 152

Recruiting job candidates, 169

Red Bull, 29, 157

Red Cross, 174, 218

Refugee travel ban, 106

REI, 19

Relationship Era (mid-20th century to mid-1990s), 68–70

Renjen, Punit, 176

RepTrak. *See* Global RepTrak methodology

Reputation: as always in a state of flux, 185; benefits of measuring, 185; Global RepTrak's method for measuring, 182*fig*–184; Unilever approach to measuring, 185

Reputation Institute, 183, 187, 210, 216

Reveal your personality, 109–110*fig*

Rometty, Ginni, 32

Room to Read, 128

Rose Global, 40, 101

Rural Airband Initiative (Microsoft), 17

S

Sales Era (1920s–1940s), 67*fig*–68

Salesforce: on *Fortune's* "Best Companies to Work For" list, 172; Marc Benioff's leadership of, 51, 166, 172; 1-1-1 model of, 51; standing against North Carolina's "bathroom law," 106; volunteer work by employees of, 166

SAS, 33, 51

Savage Arms, 19

Save the Children, 128

Schultz, Howard, 175

Scudamore, Brian, 176

Search technology, 25

Sentiment analysis tools, 187–188

Services: false claims about, 27–30, 93–94; Moral DNA exercise on playing forward, 17, 49; take a stand to ensure positivity of your, 18–20

Seventh Generation, 50

Shared Value Initiative, 9

Siemens' net zero carbon footprint goal, 137–138